# THE SUPPER CLUB

Kid-friendly meals the whole family will love

SUSIE COVER

PHOTOGRAPHY BY
CON POULOS

weldon**owen**

# Contents

## I know how hard it can be

to get your whole family around the table at dinnertime. I am a working mother with twin girls, and my husband and I are both small business owners. Before I started my own family, I was a caterer, and then I worked for several years as a private chef for a family with small children. During my time as a family chef, I learned how important it is to create wholesome dishes that both children and adults like.

## My daily goal was simple: a nutritious dinner that appealed to everyone at the table.

That task proved a challenge, but it was one I approached with gusto.

Eventually, I partnered with that family to create Susie's Supper Club. We wanted to share our experience and discoveries with others by providing solutions to families grappling with how to sit down, together, to a wholesome dinner. For two years, we operated a meal-delivery service in New York. Our success encouraged us to expand our reach. We have now launched a line of frozen food products (our four top sellers, all included here) in retail grocery stores.

With this book, I hope to continue sharing what I've learned by showing you how easy and fun it is to make these meals at home. My motto is "No fear! It's simply supper." Try the recipes and chances are you'll surprise your family—and maybe even yourself—with just how delightful and delicious home-cooked meals can be.

*Susie Cover*

# FEEDING YOUR FAMILY THE SUSIE'S SUPPER CLUB WAY

The most important basic tenet we've learned at Susie's Supper Club is that family dinnertime should never be stressful. Because we all face myriad challenges on any given day, an angst-free supper, at which everyone comes together and celebrates one another, is a worthy and noble goal.

Of course, that goal is easier said than done. We hope this book will be your guide to using good food to gather your family—whatever its makeup—at the table, even if only once a week. At Susie's Supper Club, we believe families who eat together and talk during dinner generally do better in all aspects of their lives. Turn off the telephones, televisions, computers, and whatever else distracts and make real time to visit, share stories, and eat.

Pick and choose from our collection of over one hundred recipes, each developed with all ages in mind. Involve your family in both planning and cooking the meals. For example, gather everyone together on Sunday to create menus for the coming week. If you give kids some power in deciding what the family eats, they are less likely to become picky eaters. Designing nutritious meals together at home will also influence your kids' food choices when they are out of your reach. Cook with your children on weekends, too, when everyone has more time to enjoy the experience and learn from it.

We all have days when picking up prepared food on the way home, or ordering in, is the only way to put dinner on the table. But once you start making your own easy, fun, and nutritious meals with fresh, wholesome ingredients, you probably won't want to opt for takeout unless you have to. Teach your kids how to eat just as you teach them how to say "please" and "thank you," and good eating, just like good manners, will soon be second nature. Most important, enjoy each other, listen to each other, and love each other. There is no better recipe than that.

# A Week of Wholesome Meals

A simple dinner on a busy weeknight might mean tacos and an easy dessert, or a hearty soup and a green salad. Weekends are wonderful for more leisurely cooking: roasting meats or poultry, making pizza dough, baking cookies—recipes that will yield leftovers, like roasted chicken or flank steak for sandwiches. With a little advance planning, you can keep your pantry and freezer stocked with staples, minimizing the need to shop daily. Mix and match the recipes in this book to create menus. Here is a week of delicious, family-friendly meals to get you started.

## Sunday

*Main Meal*

**ROASTED TOMATO SOUP**
19

**FLANK STEAK WITH CHIMICHURRI SAUCE**
78

**ZUCCHINI FRITTERS**
143

*Dessert*

**LEMON MOUSSE**
178

## Wednesday

*Main Meal*

**MEDITERRANEAN CHOPPED SALAD**
24

**TOMATO-MOZZARELLA LASAGNE**
119

*Dessert*

**SUMMER COBBLER**
172

## Thursday

*Main Meal*

**ROAST CHICKEN**
60

**ROASTED BABY POTATOES**
131

**HARICOTS VERTS WITH LEMON**
151

*Dessert*

**SSC BROWNIES**
162

# MONDAY

## *Main Meal*

**MISO COD**
94

**PONZU BOK CHOY**
157

**FARRO WITH FRESH CORN
AND SUGAR SNAP PEAS**

154

## *Dessert*

**APPLE PIE BARS**
168

# TUESDAY

## *Main Meal*

**CHICKEN MILANESE**
63

**POLENTA FRIES WITH KETCHUP**
128

**SPINACH SQUARES**
124

## *Dessert*

**OATMEAL CRANBERRY
COOKIES**
166

# FRIDAY

## *Main Meal*

**MINI MEAT LOAVES**
81

**QUINOA CAKES**
158

**ROASTED ASPARAGUS**
149

## *Dessert*

**FROZEN FRUIT POPS**
181

# SATURDAY

## *Main Meal*

**SALMON KEBABS**
100

**MEYER LEMON GNOCCHI**
120

**SSC CAESAR SALAD**
29

## *Dessert*

**MINI CHOCOLATE CUPCAKES
WITH SSC FROSTING**
171

# Soups & Salads

Pea Soup  16

Chicken Coconut Soup  18

Roasted Tomato Soup  19

Old-Fashioned Chicken Soup  21

Classic Vichyssoise  22

Carrot-Ginger Soup  23

Mediterranean Chopped Salad  24

Chinese Chicken Salad  26

Chef's Salad  27

SSC Caesar Salad  29

# PEA SOUP

*Serves 4-6*

This soup exploits spring's vivid fresh peas, but you can also make it with frozen organic baby peas in other seasons. Peas are a starchy vegetable; that's what makes them sweet and this soup so delicious and filling. Nourish the whole family at lunchtime, or at dinner with a big green salad alongside.

¼ cup (2 fl oz/60 ml) canola oil

4 shallots, chopped

2 Yukon gold potatoes, peeled and cut into ½-inch (12-mm) dice

2 tsp kosher salt

3½ cups (28 fl oz/875 ml) vegetable stock

3½ cups (28 fl oz/875 ml) water

6 cups (2 lb/1 kg) fresh shelled English peas or thawed frozen petite peas

¼ cup (2 oz/60 g) crème fraîche or sour cream (optional)

1  Heat the canola oil in a large saucepan over medium heat. Add the shallots and cook, stirring often, until softened and translucent, about 5 minutes. Add the potatoes, sprinkle in the salt, and stir and toss until the ingredients are well distributed and the potatoes are evenly coated with the oil.

2  Add the stock and water and bring to a simmer. Adjust the heat to maintain a low simmer and cook until the potatoes are tender, about 10 minutes. If using fresh peas, add 5 minutes from the end of cooking time, stir once, and simmer with the potatoes. If using thawed frozen peas, add at the end of cooking time, stir once, and remove from the heat. Let cool slightly. With a slotted spoon, scoop out 12–18 peas to use as garnish.

3  Transfer the soup in batches to a blender or food processor and process to a smooth purée. Pour the purée through a fine-mesh sieve back into the saucepan, pressing on the solids in the sieve with a wooden spoon to extract as much liquid as possible. Discard the solids.

4  Place the soup over low heat. Taste and adjust the seasoning. Ladle into warmed bowls, top each serving with a swirl of crème fraîche, if using, a few peas, and serve. Or, refrigerate until well chilled, at least 4 hours or up to overnight, and serve with the toppings.

# CHICKEN COCONUT SOUP

*Serves 4–6*

Our version of this classic Thai dish is less spicy than the original, and it includes two familiar ingredients the whole family will love: chicken and sugar snap peas. The lean protein from the chicken and the healthy fatty acids in coconut milk—which the body quickly turns to energy—give the soup a heartiness that will fill you up and keep you satisfied longer.

**1 tsp canola oil**

**1 tbsp peeled and minced fresh ginger**

**1 tbsp minced garlic**

**1 tbsp peeled and minced lemongrass, tender midsection only**

**2 cans (14 fl oz/430 ml each) coconut milk**

**2 tbsp sugar**

**Grated zest and juice of 2 limes**

**1½ cups (12 fl oz/375 ml) chicken stock**

**2 boneless, skinless chicken breast halves, cut crosswise into slices about ¼ inch (6 mm) thick**

**2 cups (10 oz/315 g) snow peas, trimmed and any strings removed**

**Salt and freshly ground pepper**

**See recipe photo on page 17**

**1** Heat the oil in a large saucepan over medium heat. Add the ginger, garlic, and lemongrass and sauté until softened and aromatic, about 2 minutes.

**2** Add the coconut milk and bring to a simmer. Stir in the sugar, lime zest and juice, and stock. Add the chicken, return to a simmer, and cook, stirring occasionally, until the chicken is opaque throughout, about 10 minutes.

**3** Meanwhile, bring a small saucepan filled with water to a boil over high heat and have ready a bowl of ice water. Add the peas to the boiling water and cook until tender-crisp, about 2 minutes. Using a slotted spoon, transfer immediately to the ice water to stop the cooking. When cool, drain thoroughly in a colander and pat dry. Set the peas aside.

**4** Season the soup with salt and pepper. Ladle into bowls, garnish with the peas, and serve.

# ROASTED TOMATO SOUP

*Serves 4–6*

Tomatoes are high in antioxidants, making them a healthy and delicious choice for family meals. Roasting the tomatoes imparts an intense flavor and deep red color. Omit the cream for a lighter version, if you like. This soup also freezes beautifully; stored for up to 2 months in an airtight container in the freezer, you will still be impressed by how much flavor it retains.

**2 cans (28 oz/875 g each) plum tomatoes, preferably San Marzano, drained, juices reserved**

**¼ cup (2 oz/60 g) firmly packed golden brown sugar**

**4 tbsp (2 oz/60 g) unsalted butter**

**3 shallots, finely chopped**

**1 tbsp tomato paste**

**1 tbsp all-purpose flour**

**4 cups (32 fl oz/1 l) vegetable stock**

**½ cup (4 fl oz/125 ml) heavy cream**

**1 tsp kosher salt**

**½ tsp freshly ground pepper**

**See recipe photo on page 17**

1 Preheat the oven to 400°F (200°C). Line a rimmed baking sheet with parchment paper. Spread the tomatoes in a single layer on the prepared baking sheet, and sprinkle evenly with the brown sugar.

2 Roast until the juices have evaporated and the tomatoes begin to caramelize, about 20 minutes. Remove from the oven and let cool.

3 Melt the butter in a large saucepan over medium-low heat. Add the shallots and tomato paste and cook, stirring occasionally, until the shallots are softened, about 5 minutes. Sprinkle in the flour and stir to incorporate. Cook, stirring, until thickened and the raw flour taste is gone, about 2 minutes. Slowly pour in the stock and the reserved tomato juices, whisking constantly to prevent lumps from forming.

4 Add the roasted tomatoes, raise the heat to medium-high, and bring to a boil. Return the heat to medium-low and simmer until the tomatoes are tender and breaking apart, 10–15 minutes. Remove from the heat and let cool slightly.

5 Transfer the soup in batches to a blender or food processor and process to a smooth purée, or use an immersion blender in the pan. Return to the saucepan, place over low heat, and stir in the cream, salt, and pepper. Taste and adjust the seasoning. Ladle into bowls and serve.

# OLD-FASHIONED CHICKEN SOUP

*Serves 4–6*

Packed with nutrients, this quick-fix winter soup is so easy and tasty that you may never again consider canned. Homemade or all-natural store-bought stock will add the best possible flavor and plenty of vitamins and minerals, comforting sore throats and sniffles and warding off sick days.

**6 cups (48 fl oz/1.5 l) chicken stock**

**1 boneless, skinless chicken breast half**

**2 carrots, peeled, quartered lengthwise, and thinly sliced crosswise**

**¼ cup (⅓ oz/10 g) chopped fresh dill, plus small sprigs for garnish**

**Kosher salt and freshly ground pepper**

1 In a large saucepan, bring the stock to a simmer over medium-high heat. Add the chicken and poach until opaque throughout, 15–20 minutes. Remove from the heat. Using tongs, transfer the chicken to a plate and let cool. Reserve the cooking liquid.

2 When the chicken is cool enough to handle, shred it with your fingers. Strain the cooking liquid through a fine-mesh sieve into a clean saucepan and return to a simmer over medium-high heat. Add the carrots and cook just until tender, 5–7 minutes.

3 Add the shredded chicken and dill, stir gently, and heat through. Season to taste with salt and pepper. Ladle into bowls, garnish with the dill sprigs, and serve.

# CLASSIC VICHYSSOISE

*Serves 4–6*

This summertime favorite is claimed by both the French and the Americans, but regardless of origin, it is a smooth and satisfying dish that delivers a good dose of fiber along with great flavor. Serve chilled in summer with a dollop of tangy crème fraîche, or hot in winter with a scattering of whole-wheat croutons.

**6 tbsp (3 oz/90 g) unsalted butter**

**3 leeks, white and light green parts only, thinly sliced**

**4 Yukon gold potatoes (about 1¼ lb/625 g), peeled and thinly sliced**

**6 cups (48 fl oz/1.5 l) chicken stock or water**

**1 cup (8 fl oz/250 ml) heavy cream**

**Kosher salt**

**¼ cup (2 oz/60 g) crème fraîche**

**2 tbsp finely chopped fresh chives**

1 Melt the butter in a large saucepan over medium heat. Add the leeks and cook, stirring often, until softened and translucent, about 5 minutes. Add the potatoes and toss and stir to coat with the melted butter.

2 Add the stock and bring to a simmer. Adjust the heat as needed to maintain a low simmer and cook, uncovered, until the potatoes are very tender, about 20 minutes. Remove from the heat and let cool slightly.

3 Transfer the soup in batches to a blender or food processor and process to a smooth purée, or use an immersion blender in the pan. Pour the purée into a large bowl and stir in the cream. Let cool completely, cover, and refrigerate until well chilled, at least 4 hours or up to overnight. Taste and season with salt.

4 Ladle the soup into chilled bowls. Garnish each serving with a dollop of crème fraîche and a sprinkling of chives and serve.

# Carrot-Ginger Soup

*Serves 4–6*

Thanks to a generous measure of orange-hued carrots, this beautiful, luscious soup is loaded with both vitamin A and antioxidant compounds. The flavor is an appealing mix of sweet (carrots) and spicy (ginger), and the thick consistency of a root vegetable purée will satisfy carnivores and vegetarians alike.

**¼ cup (2 fl oz/60 ml) canola oil**

**1 large yellow onion, chopped**

**4 cloves garlic, minced**

**¼ cup (1¼ oz/37 g) peeled and minced fresh ginger**

**5 large carrots, peeled and thinly sliced**

**Grated zest of 1 lemon**

**4 cups (32 fl oz/1 l) vegetable stock or water, plus more if needed**

**1 tsp kosher salt**

**½ tsp ground white pepper**

1 Heat the oil in a large saucepan over medium heat. Add the onion and cook, stirring often, until translucent, about 5 minutes. Add the garlic and ginger and sauté until softened and aromatic, about 2 minutes.

2 Add the carrots and lemon zest and cook, stirring occasionally, until the carrots begin to soften, about 5 minutes. Add the stock and bring to a simmer. Stir in the salt and adjust the heat as needed to maintain a low simmer. Cook, uncovered, until the carrots are tender, 15–20 minutes. Remove from the heat and let cool slightly.

3 Transfer the soup in batches to a blender or food processor and process to a smooth purée, or use an immersion blender in the pan. Return to the saucepan if necessary, place over low heat, and stir in the pepper. Taste and adjust the seasoning. Ladle the soup into bowls and serve.

# Mediterranean Chopped Salad

*Serves 4–6*

Loaded with a garden's worth of vegetables—bell peppers, tomatoes, cucumbers, greens—and dressed with a bright lemon-oregano vinaigrette, this salad is a hearty meal-in-a-bowl. The addition of chickpeas gives it protein and fiber for more energy throughout the day, and a big dose of folate, a water-soluble B vitamin that helps build and maintain new cells.

**LEMON-OREGANO VINAIGRETTE**

**Grated zest of 3 lemons**

**Juice of 4 lemons**

**⅓ cup (1 oz/30 g) dried oregano**

**2 tbsp Dijon mustard**

**1 heaping tbsp grated Parmesan cheese**

**2 tsp kosher salt**

**½ tsp freshly ground black pepper**

**½ cup (4 fl oz/125 ml) olive oil**

**4 cups (4 oz/125 g) loosely packed baby arugula**

**6 plum tomatoes, seeded and diced**

**2 red bell peppers, seeded and diced**

**1 English cucumber, seeded and diced**

**1 red onion, diced**

**½ lb (250 g) fresh mozzarella cheese, diced**

**1** To make the vinaigrette, combine the lemon zest and juice, oregano, mustard, Parmesan, salt, pepper, and olive oil in a jar, cover tightly, and shake vigorously until emulsified. Alternatively, whisk together all of the ingredients in a bowl until emulsified. Taste and adjust the seasoning. Set aside. (The dressing can be made up to 1 week in advance and stored in a tightly covered jar in the refrigerator.)

**2** Place the arugula in a large serving bowl. In a second large bowl, combine the tomatoes, bell peppers, cucumber, onion, and mozzarella and toss gently to mix. Pour about ¾ cup (6 fl oz/180 ml) of the vinaigrette over the vegetable mixture and toss gently again to coat thoroughly. Taste and add a little more vinaigrette, if needed.

**3** Add the vegetable mixture to the serving bowl with the arugula, toss gently to combine, and serve.

# CHINESE CHICKEN SALAD

*Serves 4-6*

A favorite among the moms who frequent our shop, this salad is easily customized by the home cook. The sweet sesame dressing, crunchy napa cabbage, and crispy fried wonton strips provide contrasting textures and flavors that will keep you satisfied and lessen any post-meal cravings. Wonton skins can be found in the frozen or Asian section of most grocery stores and delis.

½ cup (4 fl oz/125 ml) plus 1½ tbsp canola oil

5 wonton skins, cut into strips ½ inch (12 mm) wide

Kosher salt and freshly ground pepper

2 boneless, skinless chicken breast halves

1 head napa cabbage, halved lengthwise, cored, and sliced crosswise

4 green onions, white and tender green parts only, thinly sliced

¼ cup (1 oz/30 g) black sesame seeds

¼ cup (⅓ oz/10 g) finely chopped fresh cilantro

Sesame-Lime Vinaigrette (page 185)

1 Heat the ½ cup canola oil in a small nonstick frying pan over medium-high heat until just rippling. Test with a wonton strip, which should brown in about 30 seconds. Add the wontons and fry, using tongs to turn often, until lightly golden on both sides, 2–3 minutes total. Transfer to paper towels to drain and sprinkle generously with salt. Set aside.

2 Build a hot fire in a charcoal grill, preheat a gas grill to high, or preheat a grill pan until smoking. Make sure the grill rack is well scrubbed, and brush the rack or grill pan lightly with oil. Meanwhile, using a sharp chef's knife, cut each chicken breast half horizontally into 3 thin slices. Drizzle on both sides with the remaining 1½ tbsp canola oil and sprinkle with 1 teaspoon salt and ½ tsp pepper.

3 Arrange the chicken slices on the grill rack or in the pan and grill, turning once, until cooked through, about 3½ minutes per side. Transfer to a plate.

4 To assemble the salad, in a large serving bowl, combine the cabbage, chicken, green onions, sesame seeds, 2 tsp salt, and 1 tsp pepper. Set aside 1 tbsp of the cilantro and add the rest to the bowl. Pour about 1 cup (8 fl oz/250 ml) of the vinaigrette over the salad and toss to coat thoroughly. Taste and adjust the seasoning, and add more vinaigrette, if needed. Pile the crispy wontons on top of the salad, sprinkle with the reserved cilantro, and serve.

# CHEF'S SALAD

*Serves 6–8*

This salad is all about a no-cook solution for lunch or dinner. Prep the ingredients and make the dressing ahead of time, so come 5 o'clock all you have to do is assemble and serve. Ask the person behind the counter at your local gourmet deli to slice the meats ¼ inch (6 mm) thick, so they are uniform.

**6 large eggs**

**½ lb (250 g) cooked ham, thickly sliced**

**½ lb (250 g) salami, such as Genoa, thickly sliced**

**½ lb (250 g) roasted turkey, thickly sliced**

**1 lb (500 g) Emmentaler or Swiss cheese, thickly sliced**

**1 large head romaine lettuce, cored**

**2 cups (12 oz/375 g) cherry tomatoes, halved**

**Creamy Parmesan Dressing (page 185)**

1  Put the eggs in a saucepan and add cold water to cover by 1 inch (2.5 cm). Place over medium-high heat and bring just to a boil. Remove from the heat, cover, and let the pan sit undisturbed for about 8 minutes. Transfer the eggs to a colander and peel under cold running water. Chop the eggs as you would for egg salad, or slice them for a more elegant presentation.

2  Cut the ham, salami, turkey, and cheese slices into strips ¼ inch (6 mm) wide and 2 inches (5 cm) long. Put each meat and the cheese into separate bowls. Cut the romaine leaves crosswise into ribbons ½ inch (12 mm) wide.

3  To assemble the salad, put the romaine ribbons on a large platter or in a large, shallow bowl. Top the romaine with each meat, the cheese, and the egg, keeping them in separate, uniform sections and arranging them as desired. Pile the tomatoes in the middle. Serve the salad and pass the dressing at the table.

# SSC Caesar Salad

*Serves 6–8*

This beloved classic comes alive with our homemade Caesar dressing, separating it from the many lesser variations out there. Homemade wins hands down over a bottled dressing because its fresh combination of flavors—herbs, oils, spices—complements the crunchy romaine perfectly. This recipe skips the anchovies and coddled eggs for a more family-friendly version.

**CAESAR DRESSING**

**1 cup (4 oz/125 g) grated Parmesan cheese**

**3 cloves garlic, coarsely chopped**

**¼ cup (2 oz/60 g) Dijon mustard**

**¼ cup (2 fl oz/60 ml) fresh lemon juice**

**1 tsp kosher salt**

**½ tsp freshly ground pepper**

**1 cup (8 fl oz/250 ml) olive oil**

**½ baguette, preferably slightly stale, cut into ½-inch (12-mm) cubes**

**Kosher salt and freshly ground pepper**

**¼ cup (2 fl oz/60 ml) olive oil**

**4 hearts of romaine, leaves separated and large leaves torn**

**½ cup (1½ oz/45 g) Parmesan cheese shavings**

1  To make the dressing, in a blender, combine the cheese, garlic, mustard, lemon juice, salt, and pepper and blend on high speed to mince the garlic and mix well. With the machine running on low speed, slowly add the oil in a thin stream and blend until emulsified. Taste and adjust the seasoning. Set aside. (The dressing can be made up to 1 week in advance and stored in a tightly covered jar in the refrigerator.)

2  Preheat the oven to 400°F (200°C).

3  Spread the bread cubes in a single layer on a rimmed baking sheet. Season with salt and pepper, drizzle with the oil, and toss to coat, then spread again into a single layer. Bake until golden brown and crisped, about 10 minutes.

4  To assemble the salad, place the romaine and croutons in a large, shallow bowl. Pour about 1 cup (8 fl oz/250 ml) of the dressing over the salad and toss well to coat all of the romaine generously and evenly. Add a little more dressing, if needed. Garnish with the Parmesan shavings and serve.

# Sandwiches & Snacks

Roast Beef with Caramelized Onions
on Toasted Brioche 32

Roasted Turkey Wraps with
Green Apples and Brie 35

Grilled Chicken Pitas with
Roasted Tomatoes 36

Italian Vegetable Sandwiches 37

Crustless Mini Quiches 38

Spanish Tortilla Snacks 41

Trio of Crostini 42

Fresh Vegetable and Hummus Sandwiches
on 7-Grain Bread 44

Hummus and Dippers 45

Spinach Cheese Straws 47

Soft Pretzels with Honey Mustard 48

Guacamole with Homemade Tortilla Chips 51

Spiced Popcorn Two Ways 52

Potato Chips with Creamy Blue Cheese Dip 55

Homemade Granola 56

# ROAST BEEF WITH CARAMELIZED ONIONS ON TOASTED BRIOCHE

*Serves 4*

We all need a comforting treat now and again. This sandwich—with its sweet caramelized onions, heady blue cheese, and piquant horseradish sauce—is so yummy and satisfying that you will find it difficult to share it with anyone. For a more healthful sandwich, use freshly roasted turkey in place of the beef.

**1 tbsp olive oil**

**1 large yellow onion, thinly sliced**

**½ cup (4 oz/125 g) sour cream**

**2 tbsp prepared horseradish, drained**

**Kosher salt and freshly ground pepper**

**4 brioche buns, split**

**1 lb (500 g) rare roast beef, thinly sliced**

**3 oz (90 g) blue cheese, crumbled (about ¾ cup)**

**1 cup (1 oz/30 g) loosely packed baby arugula**

1 Heat the olive oil in a frying pan over medium-high heat. Add the onion and stir to coat with the oil. Reduce the heat to low and cook, stirring occasionally, until the onion is tender, browned, and caramelized, about 30 minutes. Sprinkle in a little water and scrape the bottom of the pan if the onions threaten to scorch.

2 Meanwhile, in a small bowl, combine the sour cream and horseradish and mix well. Season with salt and pepper and set aside.

3 Preheat the broiler. Arrange the brioche buns, cut side up, on a rimmed baking sheet. Slip under the broiler and broil until golden, about 5 minutes. Let cool briefly, then slather the cut side of each half with about 1 tbsp of the horseradish sauce.

4 To assemble the sandwiches, arrange the roast beef and then the caramelized onions, blue cheese, and arugula on the bottoms of the brioche buns, dividing them evenly. Replace the tops of the buns and press gently to help the sandwiches hold together. Cut each sandwich in half, if desired, and serve.

# ROASTED TURKEY WRAPS WITH GREEN APPLES AND BRIE

*Serves 4*

Even though its bold-flavored ingredients seem geared to a grown-up palate, most kids take to this sandwich, and introducing kids to new flavors early may prevent them from becoming picky eaters. If they turn up their noses at the spicy watercress, you can substitute lettuce or spinach. You can toast the wrap in a preheated 375°F (190°C) oven for 5–10 minutes or warm it in a panini press.

**4 whole-wheat wraps**

**4 tbsp (2 oz/60 g) honey mustard, store-bought or a mixture of equal parts honey and Dijon mustard**

**1 lb (500 g) roasted turkey, thinly sliced**

**½ lb (250 g) Brie cheese, cut lengthwise into 4 equal slices**

**1 Granny Smith apple, halved, cored, and thinly sliced**

**1 bunch watercress, tough stems removed**

1 Slather 1 side of each wrap with 1 tbsp of the honey mustard.

2 Place one-fourth of the turkey slices in the center of each wrap. Top each portion of turkey with 1 slice of cheese. Arrange the apple slices and then the watercress on top of the cheese, dividing them evenly. Gently fold over the sides of the wrap and press over the filling, tucking the edges snugly like a burrito.

3 Cut each sandwich in half on the diagonal and serve.

# GRILLED CHICKEN PITAS WITH ROASTED TOMATOES

*Serves 4*

For any meal, this pita sandwich is better than Middle Eastern takeout. With all fresh ingredients and lean and flavorful grilled chicken, this recipe proves why a home-cooked meal is always more satisfying and better for you than ordering in.

**PESTO MAYONNAISE**

**1 bunch fresh basil**

**2 cloves garlic**

**2 tbsp pine nuts, toasted**

**½ cup (4 fl oz/125 ml) olive oil**

**½ cup (2 oz/60 g) grated Parmesan cheese**

**1 cup (8 fl oz/250 ml) mayonnaise**

**4 plum tomatoes**

**2 tbsp olive oil**

**2 tbsp balsamic vinegar**

**3 cloves garlic, minced**

**Kosher salt and freshly ground pepper**

**2 boneless, skinless chicken breast halves**

**2 tbsp canola oil**

**½ head butter lettuce**

**4 pita breads, warmed**

1 To make the Pesto Mayonnaise, discard the tough stems from the basil. In a food processor or blender, combine the basil, garlic, pine nuts, and olive oil and process until smooth. Add the cheese and pulse briefly to blend. Transfer the pesto to a bowl, add the mayonnaise, and stir to mix well. Cover and refrigerate until ready to use.

2 Preheat the oven to 400°F (200°C). Cut the tomatoes in half crosswise and arrange them, cut side up, on a small rimmed baking sheet. In a small bowl, stir together the olive oil, vinegar, and garlic. Drizzle the olive oil mixture over the tomatoes and season with salt and pepper. Roast until lightly caramelized on top, about 30 minutes. Remove from the oven and let cool.

3 Build a hot fire in a charcoal grill, preheat a gas grill to high, or preheat a grill pan until smoking. Make sure the grill rack is well scrubbed, and brush the rack or grill pan lightly with oil. Meanwhile, using a sharp chef's knife, cut each chicken breast half horizontally through the thickness into 4 thin slices. Drizzle the slices on both sides with the canola oil and sprinkle with 1 tsp salt and ½ tsp pepper.

4 Arrange the chicken slices on the grill rack or in the pan and grill, turning once, until cooked through, about 3 minutes per side. Transfer to a plate.

5 To assemble the sandwiches, separate the lettuce leaves. Slit open the warmed pita breads about halfway around their circumference. Slather the inside of each pocket with about 2 tbsp of the Pesto Mayonnaise. Arrange 2 chicken slices in each pita, tuck the roasted tomatoes and lettuce leaves on top, dividing them evenly, and serve.

# ITALIAN VEGETABLE SANDWICHES

*Serves 4*

This delicious sandwich shows that having good condiments and bread on hand is key to making easier, healthier snacks and meals. Keep your pantry stocked with items like jarred artichoke hearts and roasted red peppers and all you'll need to pick up for this sandwich are arugula and portobello mushrooms.

**2 portobello mushrooms, stemmed and brushed clean**

**2 tbsp olive oil**

**2 tbsp balsamic vinegar**

**3 cloves garlic, minced**

**Kosher salt and freshly ground pepper**

**1 baguette, quartered and split**

**½ cup (4 fl oz/125 ml) Pesto Mayonnaise (page 36)**

**1 jar (12 oz/375 g) roasted red peppers, drained**

**1 jar (12 oz/375 g) artichoke hearts, drained and sliced lengthwise**

**2 cups (2 oz/60 g) loosely packed baby arugula**

1 Preheat the oven to 375°F (190°C).

2 Place the mushrooms on a rimmed baking sheet. In a small bowl, whisk together the oil, vinegar, and garlic. Drizzle the oil mixture over the mushrooms and turn to coat. Sprinkle both sides with salt and pepper. Bake until lightly golden and just tender when pierced with a small sharp knife, 20–25 minutes. Transfer to a plate and let cool, then cut into slices ½ inch (12 mm) thick.

3 Preheat the broiler. Arrange the baguette pieces, cut side up, on a clean rimmed baking sheet. Slip under the broiler and broil until golden, about 5 minutes. Let cool briefly, then slather the cut side of each piece with 1 tbsp of the Pesto Mayonnaise.

4 To assemble the sandwiches, arrange the roasted red peppers and then the artichoke hearts, mushrooms, and arugula on the bottoms of the baguette pieces, dividing them evenly. Replace the tops of the baguette and press gently to help the sandwiches hold together. Cut each sandwich in half on the diagonal and serve.

# Crustless Mini Quiches

Serves 6–8

Here's a quiche recipe that goes wheat free without skimping on flavor. We call for broccoli and Cheddar cheese, but you can trade out the broccoli for asparagus tips or halved cherry tomatoes and the Cheddar for Gruyère, Swiss, or Comté. Depending on what fillings you use, this recipe will make 36–48 savory treats. These bite-sized quiches make portion control easy and are guaranteed to disappear quickly at your next party.

**Nonstick cooking spray**

**½ head broccoli, thick stems removed and separated into florets**

**6 large eggs**

**6 large egg yolks**

**⅔ cup (5 fl oz/160 ml) whole milk**

**⅔ cup (5 fl oz/160 ml) heavy cream**

**1 tsp kosher salt**

**½ tsp ground black pepper**

**¾ cup (3 oz/90 g) shredded sharp Cheddar cheese**

1 Preheat the oven to 375°F (190°C). Lightly spray two 24-cup mini muffin pans with cooking spray or line with paper liners.

2 Have ready a bowl of ice water. Bring a saucepan of lightly salted water to a boil over high heat. Add the broccoli and blanch until bright green and softened but still crisp, about 30 seconds. Using a slotted spoon, transfer immediately to the ice water to stop the cooking. When cool, drain thoroughly and pat dry. Chop coarsely and set aside.

3 In a bowl, whisk together the whole eggs, egg yolks, milk, cream, salt, and pepper. (If you like, heat a small frying pan over medium-low heat, pour in about 1 tbsp of the mixture, and cook, stirring with a wooden spoon, just until soft curds form and are cooked through. Taste and adjust the seasoning.) Transfer to a large glass measuring pitcher.

4 Place the prepared muffin pans on 1 or 2 rimmed baking sheets to catch any drips. Add a few small pieces of broccoli and a generous pinch of cheese to each of the cups. Pour the egg mixture over the broccoli and cheese in each cup, filling as many as you can to just below the rim. Add a small piece of broccoli and a pinch of cheese to the top of each quiche.

5 Bake until the tops are puffed and just beginning to brown, about 15 minutes. Transfer to wire racks and let cool for about 5 minutes, then turn the quiches out of the pans, arrange on a platter or individual plates, and serve.

# SPANISH TORTILLA SNACKS

*Serves 4–6*

My father always loved "breakfast for dinner" and we have followed the tradition in our house, serving breakfast treats for every meal as well as snacks. This tortilla can be made ahead of time and warmed up when ready to eat. Serve it with a simple green salad for an easy but nourishing dinner.

**½ cup (3 oz/90 g) dried chorizo, cut into ¼-inch (6-mm) dice**

**2 small Yukon gold potatoes, peeled and cut into ¼-inch (6-mm) dice**

**2 shallots, minced**

**3 cloves garlic, minced**

**12 large eggs, beaten**

**¼ cup (1 oz/30 g) finely shredded fontina cheese**

**2 tsp kosher salt**

**¼ tsp cayenne pepper**

**Pinch of saffron threads**

**2 tbsp chopped fresh chives**

**1 tbsp chopped fresh thyme**

**2 tsp chopped fresh tarragon**

**2 tbsp chopped fresh flat-leaf parsley**

1 Preheat the oven to 375°F (190°C).

2 In a 9-inch (23-cm) nonstick, ovenproof frying pan, cook the chorizo over medium heat, stirring often, until the fat is rendered, about 7 minutes. Using a slotted spoon, transfer the chorizo to paper towels to drain.

3 Pour off all but about 2 tbsp of the fat in the pan. Add the potatoes, stir to coat with the fat, and cook until they begin to caramelize around the edges, about 5 minutes. Add the shallots and garlic and toss to mix. Cook, stirring, until the shallots soften, about 2 minutes. Pour in the eggs, then sprinkle in the cheese, salt, cayenne, saffron, and all of the herbs. Stir gently to mix. Reduce the heat to low and cook until the tortilla begins to set, about 3 minutes longer.

4 Transfer the pan to the oven and bake until the eggs are cooked through and the center is set, 5–7 minutes. Remove from the oven and let cool slightly. Run a rubber spatula along the edge of the tortilla to loosen it from the pan sides. Invert a flat plate over the frying pan, then invert the pan and the plate together and lift off the pan.

5 Cut into squares or wedges and serve hot.

# TRIO OF CROSTINI

Serves 6–8

Crostini are always a welcome snack. Here are three easy toppings: fresh cheese and tomatoes, herbed white beans, and thinly shaved veggies. Or, create your own combinations with what you have on hand in the vegetable drawer or the pantry.

**1 baguette**

**Olive oil, as needed**

**Kosher salt and freshly ground pepper**

**TOMATO TOPPING**

**6–8 cherry tomatoes**

**10 thin slices fresh mozzarella cheese**

**10 fresh basil leaves**

**WHITE BEAN TOPPING**

**1 can (15 oz/470 g) cannellini beans**

**2 fresh rosemary sprigs**

**1 clove garlic**

**Grated zest and juice of 1 lemon**

**½ cup (4 fl oz/125 ml) olive oil**

**ZUCCHINI TOPPING**

**½ zucchini**

**5 oz (155 g) fresh goat cheese**

**4 radishes, thinly sliced**

**10 small fresh dill sprigs**

1 Preheat the oven to 350°F (180°C). Cut the baguette into slices about ⅛ inch (3 mm) thick. Place in a large bowl, drizzle with ½ cup (4 fl oz/125 ml) olive oil, and sprinkle with 1 tsp salt. Toss to coat evenly. Arrange on a large rimmed baking sheet and bake until slightly browned and crispy, about 15 minutes.

2 To make the tomato topping, thinly slice or halve the cherry tomatoes. Place 1 mozzarella slice, 2 or 3 tomato slices, and 1 basil leaf on each of 10 baguette toasts. Finish with a drizzle of olive oil and a sprinkle of salt and pepper.

3 To make the white bean topping, rinse and drain the beans. Remove the leaves from the rosemary sprigs. In a food processor, combine the beans, rosemary, garlic, lemon zest and juice, and olive oil and process to a smooth purée. Season with salt and pepper. Spread about 1 tbsp of the bean purée on each of 10 baguette toasts and finish with a drizzle of olive oil. (Leftover purée can be tightly covered and stored in the refrigerator for up to 1 week.)

4 To make the zucchini topping, cut the zucchini lengthwise into ribbons. Spread 1 tbsp of the goat cheese on each of the remaining 10 baguette toasts. Place 1 or 2 zucchini ribbons, curling them attractively, and 2 radish slices on each toast. Finish with a drizzle of olive oil, a sprinkle of salt and pepper, and 1 dill sprig.

5 Arrange the crostini on a platter and serve.

# Fresh Vegetable and Hummus Sandwiches on 7-Grain Bread

*Serves 4*

A vegetarian delight, this sandwich is a powerhouse of nutrients. Pesto and hummus are repurposed as lean but flavorful spreads, and you'll find that you'll get a burst of uplifting energy from the fresh vegetables. Look for a top-quality 7-grain bread to deliver the perfect mix of texture and nuttiness.

**8 slices 7-grain bread**

**½ cup (4 oz/125 g) pesto, homemade (page 184) or your favorite store-bought**

**½ cup (4 oz/125 g) hummus, homemade (page 45) or your favorite store-bought**

**½ English cucumber, thinly sliced**

**2 plum tomatoes, thinly sliced**

**1 cup (1 oz/30 g) alfalfa sprouts**

1 Place the bread slices on a work surface. Slather 2 tbsp of the pesto on each of 4 slices. Spread 2 tbsp of the hummus on each of the remaining 4 slices.

2 Arrange the cucumber and then the tomatoes and sprouts on the pesto-coated bread slices, dividing them evenly. Top with the remaining bread slices, hummus side down, and press gently to help the sandwiches hold together. Cut each sandwich in half and serve.

# HUMMUS AND DIPPERS

*Serves 4–6*

When you make hummus from scratch for the first time, you will be surprised by how much better it tastes than most store-bought brands—fresh lemon juice and high-quality olive oil make the difference. This is the perfect to-go snack because it contains protein from the chickpeas and healthy fats from the tahini. Plus, with zero cooking time, it takes only minutes to prepare.

**1 can (15 oz/470 g) chickpeas, drained and rinsed**

**¼ cup (2½ oz/75 g) tahini**

**Grated zest of 2 lemons**

**3 tbsp fresh lemon juice**

**3 cloves garlic, coarsely chopped**

**1¼ tsp kosher salt**

**¼ cup (2 fl oz/60 ml) water**

**⅓ cup (3 fl oz/80 ml) olive oil**

**About 1½ lb (750 g) mixed raw vegetables such as cherry tomatoes, radishes, asparagus, sugar snap peas, and baby carrots, stemmed and trimmed**

**1** In a food processor, combine the chickpeas, tahini, lemon zest and juice, garlic, and salt and process on high speed for 30 seconds. With the machine running, add the water and then the oil in a thin stream, then continue to process until the mixture is perfectly smooth. This will take a few minutes. Taste and adjust the seasoning.

**2** Scoop the hummus into a serving bowl. Arrange the vegetables on a platter, and serve alongside the hummus. (Leftover hummus will keep, tightly covered in the refrigerator, for up to 1 week.)

# SPINACH CHEESE STRAWS

*Serves 4*

Cutting out and twisting these straws is a fun project to do as a family, with extremely gratifying results. For maximum flavor and enjoyment of all the heady aromas, the cheese straws should be eaten warm, or as close to when they come out of the oven as possible. If you like, substitute another vegetable like mashed squash or chopped cooked broccoli or kale for the spinach.

**All-purpose flour for dusting**

**1 sheet puff pastry, about ½ lb (250 g), thawed according to package directions if frozen**

**2 cups (8 oz/250 g) shredded sharp Cheddar cheese**

**1 cup (4 oz/125 g) shredded Gruyère cheese**

**1 package (10 oz/315 g) frozen spinach, thawed and squeezed to remove excess water (about 2 cups)**

**1 tsp kosher salt**

**½ tsp freshly ground pepper**

**1 large egg beaten with 1 tbsp water**

**½ cup (2 oz/60 g) grated Parmesan cheese**

1 Preheat the oven to 425°F (220°C). Line a large rimmed baking sheet with parchment paper.

2 On a lightly floured work surface, roll out the puff pastry sheet into a rectangle about 9 by 12 inches (23 by 30 cm) and ⅛ inch (3 mm) thick. Gently fold the pastry in half crosswise, just enough to mark the center line, then open flat again. Sprinkle the Cheddar and Gruyère, spinach, and salt and pepper evenly over one-half of the pastry. Fold the other side over to cover the filling, lining up the edges. Press with a rolling pin to flatten the filled pastry gently and seal the edges.

3 Using the tip of a sharp knife, trim the edges of the filled rectangle neatly, then cut crosswise into strips about ½ inch (12 mm) wide. Pick up a strip, holding one end in each hand, and give it a few twists, turning the ends in opposite directions to make a spiral-shaped straw. Place on the prepared baking sheet. Repeat to make the remaining straws, placing them about 2 inches (5 cm) apart on the pan.

4 Brush the straws lightly with the egg wash and sprinkle with the Parmesan. Bake until nicely puffed and golden brown, 20–30 minutes. Let cool for 10 minutes, then serve.

# Soft Pretzels with Honey Mustard

*Makes about 12 pretzels*

These twisted crisps are not complicated to make and are consistently yummy. Pick a rainy day and make it a project. Kids love playing with the dough and forming their own shapes, and you'll feel good feeding them a homemade snack.

1¼ cups (10 fl oz/ 310 ml) warm water (105°–115°F/40°–46°C)

1 package (2½ tsp) active dry yeast

1 tbsp sugar

1 cup (5 oz/155 g) all-purpose flour, plus more for dusting

1 tbsp kosher salt

Canola oil for greasing

¼ cup (1 oz/30 g) baking soda

1 large egg, lightly beaten

2 tsp coarse sea salt

Honey mustard for serving, store-bought or a mixture of equal parts honey and Dijon mustard

1  In a bowl, sprinkle the yeast and sugar over the warm water. Let stand until the yeast is foamy, about 5 minutes. Whisk until the yeast dissolves.

2  In a food processor, combine the flour and kosher salt and pulse to mix. With the machine running, add the yeast mixture slowly until a soft dough forms. Turn the dough out onto a lightly floured work surface and knead, sprinkling with flour as needed to prevent sticking, until smooth but still slightly sticky, about 8 minutes. Lightly grease a large bowl with oil. Put the dough in the bowl and turn to coat with the oil. Cover the bowl with a kitchen towel, place in a warm, draft-free place, and let the dough rise until it doubles in size, about 45 minutes.

3  Preheat the oven to 425°F (220°C). Bring a large pot three-fourths full of water to a boil over high heat. Meanwhile, line a baking sheet with parchment paper. Turn the dough out onto a lightly floured work surface and pat into a rectangle. Cut into 12 equal pieces. Roll 1 dough piece between your palms into a rope about ½ inch (12 mm) in diameter. Twist the rope into a pretzel shape and place on the prepared baking sheet. Repeat to form the remaining pretzels.

4  Add the baking soda to the boiling water, lower the heat slightly, and stir once. Drop in 3 pretzels and boil, turning once halfway through, for 30 seconds total. Using tongs, transfer to a wire rack to drain. Repeat the process to prepare the remaining pretzels.

5  Line the baking sheet with clean parchment and arrange the pretzels on the pan. Brush the tops lightly with the egg and sprinkle with the sea salt. Bake until the pretzels are golden brown and have a nice crust, about 15 minutes. Serve hot or the day of cooking with the honey mustard.

# GUACAMOLE WITH HOMEMADE TORTILLA CHIPS

*Serves 4*

Creamy avocado speaks for itself—this is a true crowd-pleaser for all ages, which gets even better when you make the chips yourself using corn tortillas. The bonus is that chips made from scratch contain almost zero saturated fat.

**1 cup (8 fl oz/250 ml) canola oil**

**5 corn tortillas, each cut into 8 wedges**

**Kosher salt**

**2 ripe avocados**

**1 plum tomato, halved, seeded, and finely chopped**

**¼ red onion, finely chopped**

**1 clove garlic, minced**

**¼ cup (⅓ oz/10 g) finely chopped fresh cilantro, plus a few whole leaves for garnish**

**Grated zest and juice of 1 lime**

**A few dashes of hot-pepper sauce, such as Tabasco (optional)**

**Freshly ground pepper**

1 Heat the canola oil in a large nonstick frying pan over medium-high heat until hot but not smoking. Working in batches to avoid crowding, add the tortilla pieces to the hot oil and fry, turning once, until golden brown, 1–2 minutes total. Using a slotted spoon, transfer the chips to a paper towel–lined baking sheet to drain. Sprinkle generously with salt while hot. When all the chips are fried, let cool completely.

2 Cut each avocado in half lengthwise and remove the pit but do not peel. Using a paring knife, score the avocado crosswise and lengthwise, creating ½-inch (12-cmm) cubes. Then, using a large spoon, scoop the diced flesh from the skin into a serving bowl. Add the tomato, onion, garlic, chopped cilantro, lime zest and juice, 2 tsp salt, ½ tsp pepper, and the hot-pepper sauce, if using, and toss gently with a wooden spoon or rubber spatula until the guacamole is blended but still chunky. Taste and adjust the seasoning.

3 Scatter the cilantro leaves on top of the guacamole and serve with the tortilla chips alongside.

# SPICED POPCORN TWO WAYS

Serves 4–6

If you're in the mood for something crunchy, tasty, and good for you, choose one of these flavor options for a double hit of sweet and savory. Serve warm in front of the fire or on family movie night.

**2 tbsp canola oil**

**½ cup (3 oz/90 g) popcorn kernels**

**TRUFFLE–THYME TOPPING**

**3 tbsp unsalted butter**

**1 tsp truffle salt**

**¼ tsp freshly ground black pepper**

**1 tsp minced fresh thyme**

**GARAM MASALA TOPPING**

**3 tbsp unsalted butter**

**2 tbsp firmly packed golden brown sugar**

**1 tbsp garam masala**

**1 tsp ground cinnamon**

**½ tsp kosher salt**

**¼ tsp cayenne pepper**

1 In a large saucepan with a lid, heat the oil over medium heat. Add the popcorn and stir with a wooden spoon to coat the kernels with the oil. Cover the pot, leaving the lid just slightly ajar, and cook until the kernels begin to pop, the popping quickens, and then the popping sounds have almost completely subsided, 6–8 minutes. Shake the pan frequently throughout. Remove from the heat and transfer the popped corn to a large serving bowl.

2 Meanwhile, make one of the toppings: Melt the butter in a small saucepan over medium-low heat. Whisk in the remaining ingredients for the topping of your choice. Drizzle over the bowl of popcorn, toss to coat evenly, and serve.

# POTATO CHIPS WITH CREAMY BLUE CHEESE DIP

*Serves 4*

We can't emphasize this enough: homemade potato chips are much tastier than store-bought. For the best results, have a deep-frying thermometer on hand to check the temperature of the oil, and allow the oil to return to the proper temperature between batches. For the best flavor, make the dip first and refrigerate, letting the flavors mingle, until ready to serve.

**½ lb (250 g) sharp blue cheese such as aged Gorgonzola**

**1 cup (8 fl oz/250 ml) heavy cream**

**Freshly ground pepper**

**1 tbsp finely chopped fresh chives**

**1 large russet potato**

**Canola oil for deep frying**

**Kosher salt**

1 In a blender or food processor, combine the blue cheese and cream and process until almost smooth. You want a little texture to remain. Season with pepper and stir in the chives. (Do not add salt, as the cheese is salty enough.) Cover and refrigerate until ready to serve.

2 Peel the potato, then slice paper-thin, preferably on a mandoline. The potato rounds should be transparent.

3 Pour oil to a depth of 3 inches (7.5 cm) into a large, deep frying pan and heat to 350°F (180°C) on a deep-frying thermometer. Or, test the temperature by dropping in a potato slice; it should sizzle and float to the surface immediately. Working in batches as needed to avoid crowding the pan, add the potatoes to the hot oil and fry until golden and crispy, 3–4 minutes. Using a slotted spoon or skimmer, transfer the chips to a paper towel–lined baking sheet to drain. Sprinkle with salt while hot.

4 Serve the chips on a platter or in a basket with the creamy cheese dip on the side.

# HOMEMADE GRANOLA

Makes 6 cups (2¼ lb/1.1 kg) or 16 bars

Our granola is the perfect blend of whole grains, dried fruits, honey, and maple syrup. For a heart-healthy kick, add some walnuts or sunflower seeds. Loose or as bars, it is ideal for breakfast or a quick snack. Store in a glass jar with a tight-fitting lid or other airtight container at room temperature for up to 2 weeks.

**3¼ cups (10 oz/315 g) old-fashioned rolled oats**

**½ cup (2 oz/60 g) golden flaxseed**

**1½ cups (6 oz/185 g) shredded coconut, preferably unsweetened**

**1 cup (4 oz/125 g) dried cranberries, coarsely chopped**

**⅓ cup (2½ oz/75 g) firmly packed golden brown sugar**

**3 tbsp clover honey**

**3 tbsp pure maple syrup**

**2 tbsp canola oil**

**2 tbsp pure vanilla extract**

**¾ tsp kosher salt**

**Nonstick cooking spray**

1 Preheat the oven to 400°F (200°C). Line a large rimmed baking sheet with parchment paper.

2 Spread the oats and flaxseed on the prepared baking sheet and toast in the oven until lightly golden and aromatic, about 10 minutes. Set aside and let cool.

3 In a large bowl, stir together the coconut and cranberries. In a small saucepan over low heat, combine the brown sugar, honey, maple syrup, oil, vanilla, and salt and cook, stirring constantly, until the brown sugar has completely dissolved and the mixture is a smooth syrup, about 5 minutes. Pour the syrup over the cranberries and coconut, add the toasted oats mixture, and stir and toss with a rubber spatula until the ingredients are evenly distributed and coated with the syrup.

4 To make loose granola, discard the parchment from the baking sheet you used to toast the oats and spray the pan lightly with cooking spray. Spread the oats mixture in a single layer on the pan and bake, stirring occasionally, until golden brown, about 30 minutes. Let cool.

5 To make granola bars, discard the parchment from the baking sheet you used to toast the oats and spray the pan lightly with cooking spray. Line the pan with clean parchment, then spray the paper. Spread the oats mixture over half of the baking sheet, pressing it into the sides and corners and shaping the opposite edge to form a rectangle about 1 inch (2.5 cm) thick. Bake until golden brown, about 30 minutes. Let cool until slightly warm, then cut into 16 bars. Transfer the pan to the refrigerator and let the bars set and cool completely, about 1 hour. Then, using a thin spatula, remove the bars from the pan and serve.

# Main Dishes

Roast Chicken 60

Chicken Milanese 63

Chicken Potpie 64

Chicken Tikka ala Mary 67

BBQ Chicken Paillard 68

Grilled Chicken Tacos 70

Turkey Boats 71

Turkey Meatballs 72

Pulled Pork Tacos 75

Pork Tenderloin
with Applesauce 76

Asian Skirt Steak 77

Flank Steak with
Chimichurri Sauce 78

Mini Meat Loaves 81

Beef Bourguignon 82

Mini Beef Burgers 85

Bolognese Calzone 86

Swedish Meatballs 89

Lamb Pizza 90

Lamb Kebabs with Citrus
Yogurt Dip 93

Miso Cod 94

Potato-Crusted Halibut 96

Sole Cakes with
Lemon Tartar Sauce 97

Asian Fish Cakes with Sweet
Chile Dipping Sauce 99

Salmon Kebabs 100

Shrimp Summer Rolls 103

Grilled Cod 104

Shrimp Cocktail 107

Tofu Pad Thai 108

Margherita Pizza 111

Asparagus and
Gruyère Pizza 112

Butternut Squash Pizza 114

Maple-Glazed
Tofu Skewers 115

Homemade Ravioli with Spinach
and Ricotta 116

Tomato-Mozzarella
Lasagne 119

Meyer Lemon Gnocchi 120

# ROAST CHICKEN

Serves 4–6

Here's a well-kept secret: it is easier to cook a whole chicken than to cook serving pieces. A golden roast chicken is always an impressive meal. It fills your home with heady smells, looks great on the table, and pleases all ages. This recipe yields plenty of gravy so you'll have lots for leftovers.

**1 whole chicken, about 3 lb (1.5 kg)**

**3 tsp kosher salt**

**1 tsp freshly ground pepper**

**1 orange, quartered**

**1 lemon, quartered**

**6 cloves garlic, smashed**

**4 fresh thyme sprigs, plus 1 tbsp chopped**

**2 fresh rosemary sprigs**

**4 cups (32 fl oz/1 l) chicken stock**

**4 tbsp (2 oz/60 g) unsalted butter**

**1 tbsp all-purpose flour**

**1** Preheat the oven to 375°F (190°C).

**2** Pat the chicken dry inside and out. Season the inside with 2 tsp of the salt and the pepper. Place 3 of the orange quarters, 2 of the lemon quarters, the garlic, and the herb sprigs in the cavity and cross the legs one over the other (or tie them together with kitchen string) to hold the juices inside. Tuck the wings under. Squeeze a lemon quarter over the outside of the chicken and rub the juice into the skin. Sprinkle the outside of the chicken with the remaining 1 tsp salt.

**3** Place the chicken, breast side up, in a roasting pan. Roast until the juices run clear when a thigh is pierced with a fork or an instant-read thermometer registers 160°F (71°C) when inserted into the thickest part of a thigh away from the bone, 1½–2 hours. Transfer to a cutting board, tent with aluminum foil, and let rest for 10 minutes.

**4** While the chicken is resting, pour 1 cup (8 fl oz/250 ml) of the stock into the roasting pan and stir to scrape up any browned bits from the bottom. Strain the pan juices through a fine-mesh sieve into a saucepan and place over low heat. Add the butter and the remaining 3 cups (24 fl oz/750 ml) stock and swirl the pan gently until the butter melts. Sprinkle in the flour and whisk until it dissolves and the gravy has thickened a little, 3–5 minutes.

**5** Squeeze the remaining orange and lemon quarters into the gravy and cook, stirring, until thickened but still loose, pourable, and glossy, about 5 minutes longer. The gravy should just lightly coat the back of a spoon. Stir in the chopped thyme. Taste and adjust the seasoning.

**6** Carve the chicken and arrange on a platter. Serve with the gravy.

# CHICKEN MILANESE

*Serves 4–6*

Here is a healthful but still delicious version of the usual chicken fingers. Our secrets are panko, the light and flaky Japanese bread crumbs, in the breading mix, and always choosing all-natural chicken because of its superior flavor. We use this versatile dish as a main course; sliced into strips (fingers) for dipping into ketchup, arranged on top of a salad, or tucked into sandwiches.

**MILANESE SAUCE**

**1 cup (8 fl oz/250 ml) mayonnaise**

**1 cup (8 oz/250 g) sour cream**

**Grated zest and juice of 2 lemons**

**1 tsp kosher salt**

**4 large eggs**

**4 cups (6 oz/185 g) panko bread crumbs**

**½ cup (2 oz/60 g) grated Parmesan cheese**

**Grated zest of 2 lemons**

**1 tbsp dried oregano**

**Kosher salt and freshly ground pepper**

**1 cup (5 oz/155 g) all-purpose flour**

**4 boneless, skinless chicken breast halves**

**Canola oil for frying**

1 To make the sauce, in a bowl, combine the mayonnaise, sour cream, lemon zest and juice, and salt and stir to mix well. Set aside.

2 Crack the eggs into a large, shallow bowl and beat until blended. In a second large, shallow bowl, stir together the bread crumbs, Parmesan, lemon zest, oregano, 1 tsp salt, and ½ tsp pepper. In a third bowl, whisk together the flour, 1 tsp salt, and ½ tsp pepper.

3 Using a sharp chef's knife, cut each chicken breast half horizontally into 3 slices. Place each slice between 2 sheets of plastic wrap and, using the flat side of a meat pounder or a small, heavy frying pan, pound to a uniform thickness of about ¼ inch (6 mm). Coat each slice first with the seasoned flour, then in the eggs, and finally in the bread-crumb mixture, shaking off any excess as you go and placing the coated pieces on a plate.

4 Pour oil to a depth of ½ inch (12 mm) into a large nonstick frying pan and heat over medium-high heat until hot but not smoking. Working in batches as needed to avoid crowding, add the chicken pieces to the hot oil and fry until golden brown and crispy on the first side, about 3 minutes. Turn and cook until golden on the second side, 2–3 minutes longer. Using tongs, transfer to paper towels to drain. Sprinkle with salt.

5 When all of the chicken is cooked, serve it piping hot with the sauce.

# Chicken Potpie

*Serves 6*

We make this dish with a puff-pastry top that is baked separately and then placed on top of the filling just before serving for a fun and unexpected presentation. You can vary the filling with different vegetables: spring asparagus, summer corn, or a medley of wild mushrooms in the fall.

8 cups (64 fl oz/2 l) chicken stock

2 lb (1 kg) boneless, skinless chicken breasts

3 slices bacon, cut into ½-inch (12-mm) dice

6 tbsp (3 oz/90 g) unsalted butter

1 large yellow onion, finely chopped

¼ cup (1½ oz/45 g) all-purpose flour

2 carrots, peeled and finely diced

1 small head celery root, peeled and finely diced

1½ cups (12 oz/375 g) sour cream

Kosher salt and freshly ground pepper

¾ cup (4 oz/125 g) fresh or frozen petite peas

1 sheet puff pastry, about ½ lb (250 g), thawed according to package directions if frozen

1 large egg beaten with 1 tbsp water

1  In a saucepan, bring the stock to a boil over high heat. Reduce the heat to medium-low, add the chicken, and simmer gently until cooked through, about 20 minutes. Using tongs, transfer the chicken to a plate and let cool. Reserve the stock.

2  While the chicken is poaching, in a large, heavy-bottomed saucepan, cook the bacon over medium-high heat until golden brown and crispy, 5–7 minutes. Using a slotted spoon, transfer to paper towels to drain.

3  Pour off all but about 1 tbsp of the bacon fat in the pan and reduce the heat to medium-low. Add the butter and let melt, then add the onion and stir to coat. Cook until the onion is translucent, about 10 minutes. Sprinkle in the flour and cook, stirring constantly, for 1 minute. Add the reserved stock, the carrots, and the celery root and bring to a simmer. Poach the vegetables until tender when pierced with a knife, about 10 minutes.

4  Pull the cooled chicken into large bite-sized pieces and add to the pan with the vegetables. Add the sour cream and the bacon and stir to mix well. Season with 2 tsp salt and 1 tsp pepper. Return to a simmer and cook until the filling has reduced by one-half, about 10 minutes. Add the peas during the last minute of cooking.

5  About 20 minutes before the filling is ready, preheat the oven to 400°F (200°C). Line a baking sheet with parchment paper. Cut the puff pastry sheet into 6 pieces, each about 2 by 3 inches (5 by 7.5 cm). Arrange the pieces on the parchment. Brush with the egg wash and sprinkle with salt. Using a fork, poke a few holes in each piece to prevent blistering. Bake until golden brown and puffy, about 10 minutes.

6  Divide the filling among warmed bowls, top each with a piece of puff pastry, and serve.

# Chicken Tikka ala Mary

*Serves 4-6*

Add a bit of international flavor to your cooking repertoire. We consider ourselves lucky that Mary May gave us this recipe before she joined the Peace Corps. It is full of flavors from your spice cabinet, yet mild enough for the whole family, lusciously creamy, and beautifully colorful on the plate.

**Ginger-Yogurt Marinade (page 186)**

**4 boneless, skinless chicken breast halves, cut into 1-inch (2.5-cm) cubes**

**TIKKA SAUCE**

**2 tbsp canola oil**

**2 yellow onions, finely chopped**

**4 cloves garlic, minced**

**1 can (28 oz/875 g) plum tomatoes, preferably San Marzano, with their juices**

**2 tbsp garam masala**

**2 tsp firmly packed golden brown sugar**

**1 tsp mild chili powder**

**½ tsp ground cinnamon**

**1 cup (8 fl oz/250 ml) heavy cream**

**Kosher salt**

**Cilantro sprigs for garnish**

1  Make the marinade and transfer it to a large bowl. Add the chicken and stir to coat thoroughly. Cover and refrigerate for at least 4 hours or up to overnight.

2  Preheat the oven to 350°F (180°C). Line a rimmed baking sheet with parchment paper. Drain the chicken and pat off the excess marinade with paper towels. Transfer to the prepared baking sheet and spread in an even layer. Bake until almost cooked through but still a little pink in the center, 7–10 minutes. Remove from the oven and set aside.

3  Meanwhile, make the sauce: In a heavy-bottomed saucepan, heat the oil over medium-low heat. Add the onions and sauté until soft and starting to color, about 6 minutes. Add the garlic and cook, stirring, for 1 minute. Add the tomatoes and their juices and crush with a fork to release the flavor. Bring to a simmer and cook, stirring often, until the sauce thickens almost to a paste, 10–12 minutes. Stir in the garam masala, brown sugar, chili powder, and cinnamon and cook for 1 minute.

4  Add the cream and the chicken and stir to mix well. Season with salt. Return to a gentle simmer and cook until the chicken is opaque throughout and warmed through, 5–7 minutes. Transfer to a warmed serving dish or individual dishes, garnish with the cilantro, and serve.

# BBQ Chicken Paillard

*Serves 4–6*

This is an irresistible summer classic. Make the BBQ sauce ahead of time, then all you have to do is grill the chicken and you're ready to eat. Our BBQ sauce is tangy and sweet, made with our homemade ketchup so it has none of the preservatives of most store-bought sauces. Use leftovers for a salad or sandwich.

**BBQ SAUCE**

4 cups (2 lb/1 kg) ketchup, homemade (page 184) or your favorite store-bought

⅓ cup (3 fl oz/80 ml) cider vinegar

¼ cup (2 fl oz/60 ml) water

Juice of 1 lemon

2 tbsp Worcestershire sauce

10 dashes of hot-pepper sauce, such as Tabasco

1 tbsp Dijon mustard

1 tsp mild chili powder

3 tbsp firmly packed golden brown sugar

3 cloves garlic, smashed

1 tsp smoked paprika

1 tsp kosher salt

Canola oil for brushing

4 boneless, skinless chicken breast halves

Kosher salt and freshly ground pepper

1 To make the sauce, combine all of the ingredients in a heavy-bottomed saucepan and stir to mix well. Bring to a simmer over medium heat, reduce the heat to low, and simmer gently, stirring often, until the sauce has thickened and the flavors have blended, about 45 minutes. Remove from the heat. Remove the smashed garlic cloves and discard. Cover to keep warm.

2 Build a hot fire in a charcoal grill, preheat a gas grill to high, or preheat a grill pan until smoking. Make sure the grill rack is well scrubbed, and brush the rack or grill pan lightly with oil.

3 Using a sharp chef's knife, cut each chicken breast half horizontally into 3 slices. Place each slice between 2 sheets of plastic wrap and, using the flat side of a meat pounder or a small, heavy frying pan, pound to a uniform thickness of about ¼ inch (6 mm). Brush the chicken on both sides with oil and sprinkle with salt and pepper.

4 Lay the chicken slices on the grill rack or in the pan at a 45-degree angle to the grill's grid and sear until nicely marked, about 2 minutes. Using tongs, rotate the same side to the opposite 45-degree angle and grill until nicely marked with cross-hatching, about 1 minute longer. Turn and grill on the second side the same way until the chicken is cooked through, about 3 minutes longer.

5 Transfer the chicken to a platter, brush on both sides with the warm sauce, and serve. Pass the remaining sauce at the table. (Leftover sauce will keep, tightly covered in the refrigerator, for up to 3 weeks.)

# GRILLED CHICKEN TACOS

Serves 4–6

Kids have fun assembling these tacos, and everyone can include exactly what they like. The salt in the marinade acts as a brine to give the chicken great flavor and tenderness. Use kosher salt or sea salt, a healthier and more flavorful choice than table salt because it is less refined and contains minerals.

**Grated zest and juice of 2 limes**

**1 tbsp kosher salt**

**¼ cup (2 fl oz/60 ml) canola oil, plus more for brushing**

**2 lb (1 kg) boneless, skinless chicken breast halves**

**12 flour tortillas, about 6 inches (15 cm) in diameter**

**1 cup (8 oz/250 g) Avocado Purée (page 185)**

**1 heart of romaine lettuce, cored and cut into fine strips crosswise**

**2 plum tomatoes, coarsely chopped**

**1** In a glass bowl or baking dish or a large zippered plastic bag, combine the lime zest and juice, salt, and oil and stir or shake to mix well. Add the chicken and turn to coat evenly. Cover tightly or seal and let marinate in the refrigerator for at least 1 hour or up to overnight.

**2** Remove the chicken from the refrigerator and let stand at room temperature for about 30 minutes.

**3** Meanwhile, build a hot fire in a charcoal grill, preheat a gas grill to high, or preheat a grill pan until smoking. Make sure the grill rack is well scrubbed, and brush the rack or the grill pan lightly with oil.

**4** Remove the chicken from the marinade and pat off the excess with paper towels. Arrange the chicken on the grill rack or in the pan at a 45-degree angle to the grill's grid and sear until marked, about 2 minutes. Using tongs, rotate the same side to the opposite 45-degree angle and grill until marked with cross-hatching, about 1 minute longer. Turn and cook the same way on the second side, about 3 minutes longer. Reduce the heat and continue to cook until the chicken is cooked through, 5–9 minutes longer. Toward the end of cooking, preheat the oven to 200°F (95°C).

**5** Transfer to a cutting board and let rest for about 10 minutes. Meanwhile, wrap the tortillas in a kitchen towel and warm in the oven.

**6** Cut the chicken across the grain on the diagonal into thin slices, and pile the slices on a platter. Arrange the warmed tortillas, the Avocado Purée, and the lettuce and tomatoes on the platter or on their own plates, and serve, instructing diners to assemble the tacos.

# Turkey Boats

Serves 4–6

All of the ingredients here are easy to find at the market, and the recipe comes together quickly. Little kids like these turkey-filled cups because they can eat them with their fingers. Dress them up by garnishing with chopped or whole fresh herb leaves. These tidbits also make good party fare.

**Nonstick cooking spray**

**24 slices whole-wheat bread, crusts removed**

**2 tbsp olive oil**

**1½ lb (750 g) ground turkey, preferably dark meat**

**3 cups (24 fl oz/750 ml) tomato sauce, homemade (page 184) or your favorite store-bought**

**3 tbsp dried oregano**

**¼ cup (1 oz/30 g) grated Parmesan cheese, plus 24 shavings**

**2 tsp kosher salt**

**½ tsp freshly ground pepper**

**2 tbsp finely chopped fresh flat-leaf parsley**

1  Preheat the oven to 375°F (190°C). Lightly spray a 24-cup mini muffin pan with cooking spray.

2  Arrange the bread slices on a work surface. Using a rolling pin, flatten each piece gently. Line each cup of the prepared pan with a bread slice, using your fingers to gently press it into the bottom and up the sides, molding it to fit. Bake until toasted and lightly browned, 8–10 minutes. Remove from the oven and let cool for 5 minutes at room temperature.

3  Heat the oil in a frying pan over medium-high heat. Add the turkey and cook, breaking up the meat with a wooden spoon, until golden brown and fully cooked through, 5–7 minutes. Add the tomato sauce, oregano, grated Parmesan, salt, and pepper and stir to mix well. Taste and adjust the seasoning.

4  Spoon a heaping 2 tbsp of the filling into each toasted bread cup. Garnish each boat with a Parmesan shaving and a sprinkle of chopped parsley, arrange on a platter, and serve.

# Turkey Meatballs

Serves 6-8

Here is an SSC superstar! This family favorite is our all-time best-seller. Turkey, rich in vitamin B and zinc, is a full-flavored but lower-fat alternative to beef (use organic meat for the best flavor and benefits), and the tomato sauce puts some beta-carotene in everyone's diet. This comforting meal is fun to make with the kids: let them mix the meat mixture and shape the balls.

6 cups (48 fl oz/1.5 l) tomato sauce, homemade (page 184) or your favorite store-bought

1 cup (1½ oz/45 g) panko bread crumbs

⅓ cup (3 fl oz/80 ml) whole milk

2 lb (1 kg) ground turkey, preferably dark meat

2 large eggs, beaten

1 cup (4 oz/125 g) grated Parmesan cheese, plus more for serving

2 tbsp dried oregano

2 tsp kosher salt

1 tsp freshly ground pepper

1 tbsp olive oil, plus more if needed

Boiled spaghetti or linguine for serving (optional)

1 In a large pot, gently heat the tomato sauce over low heat. Remove from the heat and cover to keep warm.

2 Put the panko in a large bowl. Add the milk and let soak until the crumbs have absorbed the milk completely, about 5 minutes. Add the turkey, eggs, Parmesan, oregano, salt, and pepper. Using your hands or a rubber spatula, mix gently just until well combined. Do not overmix or the meatballs will be tough.

3 Roll the turkey mixture into 1-inch (2.5-cm) balls between your palms. As the balls are formed, put them on a rimmed baking sheet. Refrigerate for 10 minutes to set.

4 In a large nonstick frying pan, heat the oil over medium-high heat. Add about one-third of the meatballs and cook, turning as needed, until nicely browned on all sides, 8–10 minutes. Using a slotted spoon, transfer the meatballs to the pot of tomato sauce. Repeat to brown the remaining meatballs in 2 more batches. Place the pot over low heat and simmer until the meatballs are cooked through, 15–20 minutes.

5 Ladle the meatballs into warmed individual bowls and serve. Or, if serving with pasta, pile the pasta on a warmed platter or individual plates or in bowls, ladle the meatballs on top, and serve. Pass additional Parmesan at the table.

# PULLED PORK TACOS

Serves 4-6

These are fantastic year-round, fun for the summer patio and cozy comfort food in winter. Cutting the meat into cubes makes it cook faster than a big shoulder of pork and makes it easier to shred when it's done. Any leftover pork is great in sandwiches: layer it with shredded carrots and cucumber slices on a French roll.

1 tbsp canola oil

2 lb (1 kg) boneless pork shoulder, cut into 1-inch (2.5-cm) cubes

1 yellow onion, thinly sliced

2 cloves garlic, minced

½ cup (4 fl oz/125 ml) red wine vinegar

1 cup (8 fl oz/250 ml) chicken stock or water, plus more if needed

1 can (28 oz /875 g) plum tomatoes, preferably San Marzano, with their juices

1 large bay leaf

Kosher salt and freshly ground pepper

12 soft flour tortillas

1 cup (8 fl oz/250 ml) Avocado Purée (page 185)

1 heart of romaine lettuce, cored and cut into fine strips crosswise

2 cups (12 oz/375 g) grape tomatoes, halved

1 In a large saucepan with a tight-fitting lid, heat the oil over medium-high heat. Working in batches to avoid crowding, add the pork and sear until browned on all sides, about 5 minutes total per batch. As the pieces are ready, using a slotted spoon, transfer them to paper towels to drain. When all of the pork is browned, set aside.

2 Add the onion and garlic to the fat in the pan and sauté over medium-high heat until the onion is softened, about 5 minutes. Add the vinegar and stir to scrape up any browned bits from the pan bottom, then cook until the liquid reduces to a glaze, about 5 minutes.

3 Add the 1 cup stock and the canned tomatoes and their juices and crush the tomatoes with a fork to release the flavor. Return the pork to the pan, add the bay leaf and stir to mix well. Season with salt and pepper. Bring to a boil, then reduce the heat to maintain a very gentle simmer. Cover tightly and cook, stirring occasionally, until the sauce has thickened, the pork is tender, and the flavors have blended, 1½–2 hours. Check the pot after 1 hour and add a little more stock if the pork seems dry. Toward the end of cooking, preheat the oven to 200°F (95°C).

4 When the pork is extremely tender and falling apart, using a slotted spoon, transfer to a plate and set aside to cool. Cook the sauce until thick and concentrated, 10–15 minutes longer. Meanwhile, wrap the tortillas in a clean kitchen towel and place in the oven to warm.

5 Using your fingers or 2 forks, shred the pork. Return it to the sauce and stir until thoroughly combined. Taste and adjust the seasoning.

6 Pile the pulled pork on a platter or divide among individual plates. Arrange the warmed tortillas and accompaniments on the platter and serve, instructing diners to assemble the tacos.

# Pork Tenderloin with Applesauce

Serves 4–6

Pork tenderloin is an easy-to-prepare cut. Here, a generous marinating time and a simple pan sauce contribute to tasty, extra-moist results. This dish is perfect in autumn, when tart fresh Granny Smiths inspire homemade applesauce.

**2 pork tenderloins, about 1 lb (500 g) each, silver skin removed**

**4 cloves garlic, coarsely chopped**

**¼ cup (2 oz/60 g) Dijon mustard**

**1 tbsp pure maple syrup**

**2 tsp fresh thyme leaves, coarsely chopped**

**1 tsp freshly ground pepper**

**1 tsp kosher salt**

**1 tbsp olive oil**

**1 large yellow onion, thinly sliced**

**2 cups (16 fl oz/500 ml) apple cider**

**Applesauce, homemade (page 186) or your favorite store-bought**

1 Pat the pork dry and place in a baking dish. In a food processor, combine the garlic, mustard, maple syrup, thyme, and pepper and pulse until the mixture is well blended and smooth. Slather the pork all over with the marinade. Cover the baking dish and refrigerate for at least 4 hours or up to overnight.

2 Remove the pork from the refrigerator and let stand at room temperature for about 30 minutes.

3 Preheat the oven to 325°F (165°C). Season the pork on all sides with the salt. Heat the oil in a large frying pan over medium-high heat. Add the pork and sear, turning as needed, until golden brown on all sides, 8–10 minutes. Transfer the pork to a deep roasting pan just large enough to accommodate it and set aside.

4 Reduce the heat to medium, add the onion to the drippings in the frying pan, and sauté until softened, about 5 minutes. Pour in the apple cider and stir to scrape up any browned bits from the pan bottom. Bring to a boil, then pour the contents of the frying pan over the pork in the roasting pan.

5 Cover the roasting pan with aluminum foil and bake until an instant-read thermometer inserted into the thickest part of the tenderloin registers 150°F (65°C), 40–50 minutes. Remove from the oven, transfer to a cutting board, tent with foil, and let rest for 10 minutes.

6 Skim off any fat from the pan sauce, then place the pan on the stove top and rewarm the sauce. Cut the pork across the grain on the diagonal into thin slices, and arrange on a platter or individual plates. Spoon the pan sauce over the pork and serve with the applesauce.

# ASIAN SKIRT STEAK

Serves 4-6

The defining flavor of this dish comes primarily from the teriyaki sauce, but we add a pinch of rosemary, a drizzle of honey, and a dollop of Dijon mustard to give it a distinctive East-West palate. The bold flavors are made for the grill. Consider doubling the recipe as the steak makes great leftovers.

**2 lb (1 kg) skirt steak, trimmed of most of the fat**

**2 cups (16 fl oz/500 ml) teriyaki sauce**

**4 cloves garlic, thinly sliced**

**1 tbsp Dijon mustard**

**½ tbsp honey**

**Leaves of 1 fresh rosemary sprig**

**Canola oil for brushing**

1 Pat the steak dry. In a baking dish, whisk together the teriyaki sauce, garlic, mustard, honey, and rosemary. Add the steak and turn to coat with the marinade. Cover the dish tightly with plastic wrap and refrigerate for at least 4 hours or up to overnight.

2 Remove the steak from the refrigerator and let stand at room temperature for about 30 minutes. Build a hot fire in a charcoal grill, preheat a gas grill to high, or preheat a grill pan until smoking. Make sure the grill rack is well scrubbed, and brush the rack or the grill pan lightly with oil.

3 Remove the steak from the marinade and pat off the excess with paper towels. Place the steak on the grill rack or in the pan and grill, turning once, for about 3 minutes per side for medium-rare. Transfer to a cutting board, tent with aluminum foil, and let rest for 10 minutes.

4 Carve the steak across the grain on the diagonal into thin slices, arrange on a platter or individual plates, and serve.

# Flank Steak with Chimichurri Sauce

*Serves 4–6*

Flank steak is a good choice for family meals. Flavorful and not too expensive, this long, usually thin cut soaks up seasonings and stays tender. The fresh herbs in the Argentine sauce add not only beautiful color, but also may deliver anti-inflammatory benefits that can contribute to keeping you healthy.

**CHIMICHURRI SAUCE**

¼ cup (⅓ oz/10 g) chopped fresh flat-leaf parsley

2 tbsp chopped fresh cilantro

4 cloves garlic, coarsely chopped

1 cup (8 fl oz/250 ml) olive oil

⅔ cup (5 fl oz/160 ml) red wine vinegar

1 tsp ground cumin

1 tsp kosher salt

2 lb (1 kg) flank steak, trimmed of excess fat

2 tsp olive oil

1 To make the sauce, in a blender or food processor, combine all of the ingredients and process to a smooth purée. Reserve ½ cup (4 fl oz/125 ml) of the sauce to marinate the steak. Transfer the rest to a small serving bowl and refrigerate until ready to use.

2 Place the steak in a baking dish. Pour the reserved sauce over the steak, then turn the steak to coat completely. Cover the dish tightly with plastic wrap and refrigerate for at least 4 hours or up to overnight.

3 Remove the steak from the refrigerator and let stand at room temperature for about 30 minutes. Remove the sauce from the refrigerator at the same time to bring it to room temperature.

4 In a large nonstick frying pan, heat the oil over high heat. Remove the steak from the marinade and pat off the excess with paper towels. Add to the hot pan and sear, turning once, until browned on both sides, about 3 minutes per side for medium-rare. Transfer the steak to a cutting board, tent with aluminum foil, and let rest for 10 minutes.

5 Carve across the grain and on the diagonal into thin slices, arrange on a platter or individual plates, and serve. Pass the sauce at the table.

# Mini Meat Loaves

Serves 4–6

Here is another recipe in which we take a mainstream dish and make it miniature. These little loaves are downright pick-up-able—a happy thing, because that makes it easy to dip them in ketchup. And because they taste delicious at room temperature, they are perfect to pack for a school lunch or picnic. Free form the size as you like and use grass-fed beef or all-natural turkey whenever possible.

**½ cup (¾ oz/20 g) panko bread crumbs**

**¾ cup (6 fl oz/180 ml) whole milk**

**¾ lb (375 g) ground beef or turkey**

**¼ cup (2 oz/60 g) ketchup, homemade (page 185) or your favorite store-bought, plus more for serving**

**2 tbsp grated Parmesan cheese**

**1 tsp kosher salt**

**½ tsp freshly ground pepper**

1 Preheat the oven to 375°F (190°C).

2 Put ¼ cup (⅓ oz/10 g) of the bread crumbs in a large bowl. Add the milk and let soak until the crumbs have absorbed the milk completely, about 3 minutes. Add the beef, the remaining ¼ cup bread crumbs, the ketchup, Parmesan, salt, and pepper. Using your hands or a rubber spatula, mix gently just until well combined. Do not overmix or the meat loaves will be tough.

3 Line the baking sheet with parchment paper. Form the beef mixture into 12 mini loaves each about 3 inches (8 cm) long, 2 inches (5 cm) wide, and 1¼ inches (3 cm) high and arrange on the prepared pan 1–2 inches (2.5–5 cm) apart. Or, you can divide the meat mixture into 4–6 equal portions, and pack each portion into a nonstick mini loaf pan.

4 If baking freestanding loaves, bake until the bottoms are browned, 20–25 minutes. If using loaf pans, bake until a meat thermometer registers 160°F (71°C) inserted in the center of the loaf, about 30 minutes. Unmold the loaves, if necessary, and serve. Pass additional ketchup at the table.

# Beef Bourguignon

*Serves 4–6*

This classic "adult" dish can be appreciated by all ages. We blend our sauce to make it smooth, the way kids like it. Packed with lots of fresh herbs and a slow caramelizing in the pan, the vegetable-based sauce is rich in nutrients and flavor.

**1½ lb (750 g) boneless beef shoulder, trimmed of excess fat and cut into 1-inch (2.5-cm) cubes**

**Kosher salt and freshly ground pepper**

**¼ cup (2 fl oz/60 ml) olive oil**

**1½ cups (7½ oz/235 g) finely chopped yellow onions**

**1½ cups (7½ oz/235 g) peeled and finely chopped carrots**

**1½ cups (7½ oz/235 g) finely chopped celery**

**3½ cups (28 fl oz/875 ml) beef or chicken stock, plus more if needed**

**1 can (28 oz/875 g) plum tomatoes, preferably San Marzano, with their juices**

**2 fresh thyme sprigs**

**2 fresh rosemary sprigs**

**2 fresh flat-leaf parsley sprigs, plus ¼ cup (⅓ oz/10 g) chopped**

**1 bay leaf**

**Boiled egg noodles for serving**

1  Preheat the oven to 325°F (165°C). Pat the beef dry with paper towels and sprinkle all over with salt and pepper.

2  In a large Dutch oven or other heavy-bottomed ovenproof pot, heat the olive oil over medium-high heat. Working in batches to avoid crowding, add the beef and sear, turning as needed, until browned on all sides, about 5 minutes total per batch. As the pieces are ready, using a slotted spoon, transfer them to a plate. Set the beef aside.

3  Add the onions, carrots, and celery to the pot, stir to coat, and sauté until beginning to soften and caramelize, about 10 minutes. Add the stock and the tomatoes with their juices. Break up the tomatoes with a spoon and stir to scrape up any browned bits from the pot bottom.

4  Return the beef to the pot, along with any accumulated juices. Add the herb sprigs and bay leaf and bring to a boil. Cover and transfer to the oven. Braise until the beef is very tender, about 2 hours. Check after 1 hour; if the beef seems dry, pour in a little more stock.

5  When the beef is tender, remove the pot from the oven. Using tongs, transfer the beef to a plate and set aside. Place the pot over low heat and simmer the sauce, uncovered, until thickened, 15–30 minutes. Remove from the heat. Discard the herb sprigs and bay leaf and let the sauce cool for a few minutes.

6  Working in batches, transfer the contents of the pot to a blender and process to a coarse purée, then return to the pot. If the sauce seems too thick, add a little more stock. Return the beef to the sauce. Taste and adjust the seasoning and rewarm gently over low heat, if necessary.

7  Divide the noodles among warmed bowls and ladle the stew on top. Garnish with the chopped parsley and serve.

# MINI BEEF BURGERS

*Serves 6–8*

We love anything bite-sized at SSC—and we know kids do, too. We also know that when it comes to burgers, everyone likes to dress them differently, especially the picky eaters in your house. Offering diners fun and elegant options, from sharp Cheddar cheese to our homemade ketchup, ensures that dressing these minis "their way" produces ultimate satisfaction.

1¾ lb (875 g) ground beef

Kosher salt and freshly ground pepper

2 tbsp canola oil

9 oz (280 g) sharp Cheddar cheese, thinly sliced and cut into 2-inch (5-cm) squares (optional)

18 store-bought mini brioche buns or potato rolls, split

Ketchup, homemade (page 185) or your favorite store-bought, for serving

Condiments of choice such as pickles, mustard, butter lettuce leaves, tomato slices and/or red onion slices

1  Shape the ground beef into 18 patties each about 2 inches (5 cm) in diameter and 1½ inches (4 cm) thick. Season the patties on both sides with salt and pepper.

2  In a large nonstick frying pan, heat 2 tsp of the oil over medium-high heat. When the oil is hot, add 6 of the burgers and cook, turning once, for about 2 minutes per side for medium-rare. Remove from the heat. If using the cheese, place a piece on each burger and cover the pan for a few seconds so the cheese melts. Transfer to a platter, tent with aluminum foil, and repeat to cook the remaining burgers in batches.

3  Put the burgers between the bun halves and serve. Pass the ketchup and condiments at the table.

# BOLOGNESE CALZONE

Serves 4–6

Anything can go into these superdelicious calzone. If you have leftover vegetables in the fridge, finely chop them and stir into the beef sauce to maximize nutrition. Or, sauté them and mix into tomato sauce for a vegetarian filling.

Pizza Dough (page 183)

2 tbsp unsalted butter

Olive oil

1 yellow onion, finely chopped

1 carrot, peeled and finely chopped

2 cloves garlic, finely chopped

1½ lb (750 g) ground beef

1 tbsp tomato paste

Kosher salt and freshly ground pepper

1 cup (8 fl oz/250 ml) whole milk

Pinch of freshly grated nutmeg

¾ cup (6 fl oz/180 ml) chicken or beef stock

1 tbsp red wine vinegar

2 cans (28 oz/875 g each) plum tomatoes, preferably San Marzano, with their juices

¼ cup (1 oz/30 g) grated Parmesan cheese

2 tbsp chopped fresh basil

Cornmeal and all-purpose flour for dusting

1 Make the dough and divide into 4 equal pieces. Shape each piece into a disk, and let rise for a second time as directed.

2 In a large, heavy-bottomed saucepan, melt the butter with 2 tbsp oil over medium-high heat. Add the onion, carrot, and garlic and sauté until softened, about 3 minutes. Add the beef and cook, breaking up the meat with a wooden spoon, until browned, about 8 minutes. Add the tomato paste, 2 tsp salt, and 1 tsp pepper and cook for 1 minute.

3 Add the milk and nutmeg, stir well, and cook until most of the milk has been absorbed, about 10 minutes. Add the stock and vinegar and cook again until most of the liquid has been absorbed, about 10 minutes longer. Add the tomatoes with their juices, break up the tomatoes with a fork to release the flavor, and bring the sauce to a boil.

4 Reduce the heat to maintain a very low simmer and cook, uncovered, until the sauce is thick and flavorful, about 45 minutes. Stir in the Parmesan and basil. Taste and adjust the seasoning.

5 Preheat the oven to 400°F (200°C). Dust a large rimmed baking sheet with cornmeal.

6 On a lightly floured work surface, roll out 1 dough disk into a round about 6 inches (15 cm) in diameter and ½ inch (12 mm) thick. Scoop a heaping ¼ cup (2 fl oz/60 ml) of the Bolognese sauce in the center and fold the dough in half over the sauce to make a half-moon. Seal the edges by pressing with the tines of a fork, making a pretty border. Brush the top lightly with oil and sprinkle with salt. Place on the prepared baking sheet. Repeat to assemble the remaining calzone.

7 Bake until the tops are golden, 15–20 minutes. Let cool slightly and serve.

# Swedish Meatballs

Serves 8–10

Who can resist a beloved comfort food that comes together in under an hour? To get everyone involved, let the kids do the shaping. Grass-fed beef will create the most flavorful meatballs, ideal served over egg noodles, with a green salad.

¾ cup (3 oz/90 g) fresh bread crumbs

½ cup (4 fl oz/125 ml) whole milk

1 lb (500 g) ground beef

1 large egg, beaten

1 tsp freshly grated nutmeg

Kosher salt and freshly ground pepper

2 tbsp unsalted butter, plus more if needed

4 shallots, thinly sliced

1½ cups (12 fl oz/375 ml) beef stock

1½ cups (12 fl oz/375 ml) heavy cream

Boiled egg noodles for serving

1 tbsp chopped fresh flat-leaf parsley or dill

**1** Put the bread crumbs in a large bowl. Add the milk and let soak until the crumbs have absorbed the milk completely, 5–10 minutes. Add the beef, egg, nutmeg, 1 tsp salt, and 1 tsp pepper. Using your hands or a rubber spatula, mix gently just until well combined. Do not overmix or the meatballs will be tough.

**2** Roll the beef mixture into 1-inch (2.5-cm) balls and arrange on a rimmed baking sheet. Refrigerate for 10 minutes to set.

**3** Preheat the oven to 375°F (190°C).

**4** In a large nonstick frying pan, melt 1 tbsp of the butter over medium-high heat. Add one-third of the meatballs and sear, turning as needed, until nicely browned on all sides, about 5 minutes. Transfer to a clean baking sheet. Repeat to brown the remaining meatballs in batches. Only add more butter if the pan seems too dry; you want the meatballs to have a nice brown crust, and if there is too much liquid in the pan, they will steam. Transfer to the oven, reserving the frying pan and drippings. Bake the meatballs until cooked through, 15–20 minutes.

**5** Meanwhile, add the shallots to the drippings in the frying pan and place over medium heat. Sauté until softened, about 3 minutes, adding more butter if needed. Add the stock, raise the heat and bring to a boil. Reduce the heat to medium-low and simmer until the liquid is reduced by half, about 5 minutes. Stir in the cream and cook until the sauce has thickened and coats the back of a spoon, about 3 minutes longer. Swirl in the remaining 1 tbsp butter. Taste and adjust the seasoning.

**6** When the meatballs have finished cooking, return them to the frying pan and turn to coat with the sauce. Pile the egg noodles on a platter or individual plates and arrange the meatballs on top, spooning more of the sauce over the top. Garnish with the parsley and serve.

# LAMB PIZZA

*Makes four 6-inch (15-cm) pizzas*

These pizzas are inspired by a traditional dish served in Middle Eastern restaurants. They are an ideal way to introduce a new protein and flavor to your children, who are bound to eat them if you call them pizzas.

Pizza Dough (page 183)

2 tbsp olive oil

1½ lb (750 g) ground lamb from the leg

2 cups (8 oz/250 g) chopped yellow onion

2 cloves garlic, chopped

2 tsp chopped fresh thyme leaves

1 tsp dried oregano

3 cups (18 oz/560 g) canned plum tomatoes, preferably San Marzano, with their juices

½ cup (4 fl oz/125 ml) beef or lamb stock

1 tsp kosher salt

1 tsp freshly ground pepper

Cornmeal and all-purpose flour for dusting

1  Make the dough and let rise the first time as directed.

2  To make the topping, in a large, heavy frying pan, heat 1 tbsp of the oil over medium-high heat. Add the lamb and cook, breaking it up with a wooden spoon, until browned, about 8 minutes. Using a slotted spoon, transfer the lamb to a bowl, then discard the fat in the pan.

3  Return the pan to medium heat and add the remaining 1 tbsp oil. Add the onion and garlic and sauté until tender and lightly golden, about 8 minutes. Return the lamb to the pan, add the thyme and oregano, and cook, stirring occasionally, for 2–3 minutes. Add the tomatoes and stock and crush the tomatoes with a fork to release the flavor. Reduce the heat to low and simmer, uncovered, until most of the liquid has evaporated and the mixture is thick, about 45 minutes. Season with the salt and pepper. Remove from the heat and let cool completely.

4  Meanwhile, divide the dough into 4 equal pieces, shape each piece into a disk, and let rise for a second time as directed. Preheat the oven to 400°F (200°C). Dust 2 large rimmed baking sheets with cornmeal.

5  On a lightly floured work surface, roll out 1 dough disk into a round about 6 inches (15 cm) in diameter and ½ inch (12 mm) thick. Pinch around the edge to create a ½-inch (12-mm) rim, and place the round on one-half of a cornmeal-dusted baking sheet. Arrange one-fourth of the lamb mixture evenly over the crust, leaving the rim uncovered. Repeat to assemble the second pizza, placing it next to the first one on the other half of the baking sheet.

6  Bake until the dough is set and golden brown, 10–12 minutes. Meanwhile, assemble the remaining 2 pizzas on the second pan and slip them into the oven when the first batch is done. Cut all the pizzas into slices and serve.

# Lamb Kebabs with Citrus Yogurt Dip

*Makes 4–6*

Marinating is an important step in this recipe as it keeps the lamb tender. The tangy citrus yogurt dip would also be delicious as a healthy dip for vegetables or grilled pita points, or as a refreshing spread for sandwiches.

**2 cups (1 lb/500 g) plain yogurt**

**1½ cups (12 fl oz/375 ml) water**

**2½ lb (1.25 kg) boneless lamb shoulder, trimmed of excess fat and cut into 1-inch (2.5-cm) cubes**

**2 cloves garlic, minced**

**1½ tsp mild chili powder**

**1½ tsp kosher salt**

**1 tsp ground cumin**

**Canola oil for brushing**

**2 large red bell peppers, seeded and cut into 1½-inch (4-cm) pieces**

**3 tbsp unsalted butter, melted**

**Juice of 1 lemon**

**Citrus Yogurt Dip (page 186) for serving**

**1** In a large bowl, whisk together 1 cup (8 oz/250 g) of the yogurt with the water. Add the lamb and stir to coat thoroughly. Cover and refrigerate for at least 4 hours or up to overnight.

**2** Drain the lamb and pat off the excess marinade with paper towels. In a clean large bowl, whisk together the remaining 1 cup yogurt, the garlic, chili powder, salt, and cumin. Add the lamb, stir to coat again, and let stand at room temperature for 30 minutes. Meanwhile, soak 8–12 wooden skewers in water for 30 minutes.

**3** Build a hot fire in a charcoal grill, preheat a gas grill to high, or preheat a grill pan until smoking. Make sure the grill rack is well scrubbed, and brush the rack or the grill pan lightly with oil.

**4** Drain the skewers. Thread 3 pieces of lamb and 3 pieces of bell pepper on each skewer, starting with the lamb and alternating with the pepper. Leave the bottom 2 inches (5 cm) or so of the skewers empty to use as a handle. Whisk together the melted butter and lemon juice in a small bowl and have ready next to the grill or stove top.

**5** Arrange the skewers on the grill rack or in the pan and grill, basting with the butter mixture and turning as needed to brown on all sides, until the kebabs begin to char on the edges and the lamb cubes are a warm pink in the middle, 5–7 minutes. Serve with the dip on the side.

# Miso Cod

Serves 4

This is a mouthwatering variation on the classic dish found in many modern Asian-inspired restaurants. The marinade bath both flavors and cures the fish. Don't be afraid to try out a new taste for your family; supremely easy to make, roasted cod fillets please almost everyone, even if they think they don't like fish. If you can't find or afford the fish suggested here, ask your fishmonger to suggest penny-wise firm white fish fillets that can be substituted.

1 cup (8 fl oz/250 ml) mirin

2 cups (1 lb/500 g) white or yellow miso paste

1¼ cups (10 oz/315 g) sugar

4 black cod or other butterfish fillets, about 6 oz (185 g) each

Canola oil for greasing

1 In a small saucepan, warm the mirin over medium heat. Do not allow to boil. Add the miso and stir until completely dissolved, about 5 minutes. Add the sugar and stir until dissolved. Remove from the heat and let cool completely.

2 Pat the fillets dry. Place in a baking dish and generously slather on both sides with the miso mixture. Cover the dish with a piece of plastic wrap. Refrigerate for at least 24 hours.

3 Preheat the oven to 400°F (200°C). Lightly grease a rimmed baking sheet with oil.

4 Heat a nonstick frying pan over medium-high heat. Uncover the fish and wipe off the excess marinade with paper towels. Add the fillets to the hot pan and sear until nicely browned and caramelized on the bottom, 30 seconds to 1 minute. Be careful, as the fish will blacken quickly because of the sugar in the coating. Transfer the fillets to the prepared baking sheet, carefully turning them blackened side up. Bake until the fish is cooked through and flakes easily, about 7 minutes.

5 Transfer the fillets to a platter or individual plates and serve.

# POTATO-CRUSTED HALIBUT

*Serves 4*

This is a healthful and hearty dish all in one. Kids love it for the crispy potato crust and grown-ups love it because halibut provides omega-3 fatty acids for future brainiacs. For the best texture and the prettiest presentation, do not move the fish once it hits the pan, so that the crust sears properly.

**1 large russet potato**

**⅓ cup (3 fl oz/80 ml) mayonnaise**

**3 tbsp capers, rinsed, drained, and coarsely chopped**

**2 tbsp chopped fresh flat-leaf parsley**

**Kosher salt and freshly ground pepper**

**4 halibut fillets, about 6 oz (185 g) each**

**2 tbsp canola oil, plus more if needed**

1 Preheat the oven to 400°F (200°C). Lightly oil a shallow baking dish.

2 Peel the potato. Using the large holes on a box grater-shredder, grate the potato, then transfer to a clean kitchen towel and squeeze gently to remove any excess water. In a small bowl, combine the mayonnaise, capers, parsley, and salt and pepper to taste.

3 Pat the fish dry. Spread about 2 tbsp of the caper mayonnaise on one side of each fillet. Gently mound one-fourth of the grated potato on top of the mayonnaise on each fillet and spread in an even layer. Press the potatoes lightly to help them adhere to the mayonnaise.

4 Heat the oil in a large nonstick frying pan over high heat until very hot but not smoking. Carefully place 2 fillets, potato side down, in the hot pan and cook for 2 minutes. Press down firmly with a spatula to help the crust set, then continue cooking until the crust is golden brown and crispy, about 3 minutes longer.

5 Season the tops, or flesh side, with salt and pepper. Transfer the fillets to the prepared baking dish, carefully turning them potato side up. Repeat to encrust the remaining 2 fillets, adding more oil to the frying pan, if needed. Bake until the fish is cooked through and flakes easily, 5–7 minutes.

6 Transfer the fillets to a platter or individual plates and serve.

# SOLE CAKES WITH LEMON TARTAR SAUCE

*Serves 4–6*

A mom's dream come true: these healthful cakes, paired with roasted rosemary baby potatoes in place of fries, are the ideal stand-in for fish and chips. Feed your children good-for-them alternatives like this one and you will be amazed at how their tastes can change for the better.

**LEMON TARTAR SAUCE**

1 cup (8 fl oz/250 ml) mayonnaise

1 tbsp capers, rinsed, drained, and coarsely chopped

1 tbsp chopped fresh flat-leaf parsley

Grated zest and juice of 1 lemon

½ tsp kosher salt

1½ lb (750 g) sole fillets, cut into 1-inch (2.5-cm) pieces

1 large egg

Grated zest and juice of 2 lemons

½ cup (½ oz/15 g) panko bread crumbs, plus 1 cup (1 oz/30 g) for dredging

½ cup (2 oz/60 g) grated Parmesan cheese

1 tbsp dried oregano

Kosher salt and ground white pepper

Canola oil for frying

1 To make the sauce, in a small bowl, stir together all of the ingredients to mix well. Cover and refrigerate until ready to serve.

2 Put the fish in a food processor and pulse just until uniformly minced, about 10 times. Be careful not to overprocess or the fish will turn into a paste. Transfer to a large bowl and add the egg, lemon zest and juice, the ½ cup bread crumbs, the Parmesan, the oregano, 1 tsp salt, and ½ tsp pepper. Using your hands or a rubber spatula, gently fold and toss the ingredients together until well combined.

3 Place the 1 cup bread crumbs in a shallow dish. Shape the fish mixture into cakes about 2 inches (5 cm) in diameter and 1 inch (2.5 cm) thick. Coat each cake thoroughly with the bread crumbs, shaking off the excess.

4 Line a rimmed baking sheet with paper towels. Pour oil to a depth of ½ inch (12 mm) into a nonstick frying pan and heat over medium heat until hot and shimmering but not smoking. Working in batches as needed to avoid crowding, add the cakes, placing them about 1 inch (2.5 cm) apart, and fry, turning once, until golden brown and crispy, about 3 minutes per side. Transfer to the paper towels to drain and season generously with salt while still warm.

5 Transfer the cakes to a platter or individual plates and serve. Pass the sauce at the table.

# Asian Fish Cakes with Sweet Chile Dipping Sauce

*Serves 4–6*

These toothsome but light, zesty cakes are a great way to get everyone to like fish. You can vary the ingredient amounts in the sauce to your taste; try adjusting the garlic or ginger to bring out different flavors. Susie's Tip: These cakes freeze beautifully for up to 2 months, so make a bunch ahead of time and have them on hand for a play date that goes into dinnertime.

**2 lb (1 kg) cod fillets, cut into 1-inch (2.5-cm) pieces**

**2 large eggs**

**½ cup (½ oz/15 g) panko bread crumbs, plus 1 cup (1 oz/30 g) for dredging**

**¼ cup (⅓ oz/10 g) finely chopped fresh cilantro**

**4 green onions, white and tender green parts only, thinly sliced**

**2 tbsp peeled and grated fresh ginger**

**1 tbsp lime zest**

**2 cloves garlic, minced**

**½ tsp fish sauce**

**2 tsp kosher salt**

**1 tsp freshly ground pepper**

**Canola oil for frying**

**Sweet Chile Dipping Sauce (page 186) for serving**

1 Put the fish in a food processor and pulse just until uniformly minced, about 10 times. Be careful not to overprocess or the fish will turn into a paste. Transfer to a large bowl and add the eggs, the ½ cup bread crumbs, the cilantro, green onions, ginger, lime zest, garlic, fish sauce, salt, and pepper. Using your hands or a rubber spatula, gently fold and toss the ingredients together until well combined.

2 In a nonstick frying pan, heat a splash of oil over medium-high heat. Pinch off a small piece of the fish mixture and fry until cooked through, about 1 minute. Taste and adjust the seasoning of the remaining fish mixture if needed.

3 Place the 1 cup bread crumbs in a shallow dish. Shape the fish mixture into cakes about 2 inches (5 cm) in diameter and 1 inch (2.5 cm) thick. Coat each cake thoroughly with the bread crumbs, shaking off the excess.

4 Line a rimmed baking sheet with paper towels. Pour oil to a depth of ½ inch (12 mm) into the frying pan and heat until hot and shimmering but not smoking. Working in batches as needed to avoid crowding, add the cakes, placing them about 1 inch (2.5 cm) apart, and fry, turning once, until golden brown and crispy, 2–3 minutes per side. Transfer to the paper towels to drain and season with salt while still warm.

5 Transfer the cakes to a platter or individual plates and serve. Pass the dipping sauce at the table.

# SALMON KEBABS

*Makes 4–6*

Wild salmon is a great source of protein and omega-3 fatty acids, which are essential for a healthy heart and glowing skin. Kebabs are a simple and quick way to bring all of that goodness that salmon carries to your family. Plus, at the dinner table, kids always find anything on a stick to be fun.

**½ cup (4 fl oz/125 ml) ponzu sauce, store-bought or a mixture of ⅓ cup (3 fl oz/80 ml) soy sauce with the juice of 1 lemon**

**1 tbsp grated lemon zest**

**2 tsp fresh lemon juice**

**1 fresh rosemary sprig**

**2 lb (1 kg) salmon fillets, cut into 1-inch (2.5-cm) cubes**

**1** In a large bowl, whisk together the ponzu, lemon zest and juice, and rosemary. Add the fish and stir to coat. Cover and refrigerate for at least 4 hours or up to overnight.

**2** Soak 10 wooden skewers in water for 30 minutes.

**3** Preheat the oven to 400°F (200°C). Drain the skewers. Using a slotted spoon, transfer the fish from the marinade to a clean large bowl; reserve the marinade. Thread the cubes onto the skewers, dividing them evenly.

**4** Arrange the skewers on a baking sheet and roast until the edges begin to crisp and the fish is mostly cooked through but still orange-pink and moist on the inside, about 5 minutes total, turning once.

**5** Meanwhile, pour the reserved marinade into a small saucepan and bring to a boil over high heat. Reduce the heat to medium and cook until the sauce thickens enough to coat the back of a spoon, 2–3 minutes.

**6** Transfer to a platter or individual plates. Pour the sauce over the hot skewers and serve.

# SHRIMP SUMMER ROLLS

*Serves 4*

Great for parties, dinners with friends, or just to impress your family, these rolls are gorgeous, belying how quick and easy they are to assemble. Get creative and add different vegetables, like carrots for extra crunch, or savory leftovers, like roast chicken. Let older kids do the rolling if they want to be part of the action.

**10 oz (315 g) thin cellophane noodles or dried rice vermicelli**

**1 lemon, halved**

**1 bay leaf**

**16 large shrimp, peeled and deveined**

**1 cup (8 fl oz/250 ml) ponzu sauce, store-bought or a mixture of ¾ cup (6 fl oz/180 ml) soy sauce with the juice of 2 lemons**

**1 tbsp reduced-sodium soy sauce**

**2 tbsp chunky peanut butter**

**16 dried rice paper wrappers, 8 inches (20 cm) in diameter**

**¼ cup (1 oz/30 g) black sesame seeds**

**16 fresh mint leaves**

**16 fresh cilantro leaves**

**½ English cucumber, quartered lengthwise and cut into narrow strips**

1 Put the noodles in a bowl with very hot (not boiling) water to cover and let stand until softened, 2–3 minutes. Drain the noodles, place under cold running water, and drain again thoroughly. Set aside.

2 Fill a saucepan three-fourths full of water. Add the lemon and bay leaf. Bring to a boil over high heat, then reduce the heat to medium. Add the shrimp and poach just until cooked through, about 2 minutes. Drain immediately in a colander and place under cold running water until cool to the touch. Pat dry on paper towels and cut each shrimp in half lengthwise. Refrigerate until ready to use.

3 In a large bowl, stir together ½ cup (4 fl oz/125 ml) of the ponzu sauce, the soy sauce, and the peanut butter until smooth. Add the noodles and toss with the sauce to coat.

4 Fill a large, shallow bowl with hot water (but not too hot to touch) and place on a work surface. Put the rice papers next to the bowl. Place 1 wrapper in the hot water and soak until softened, about 30 seconds. Lay it flat on the work surface and pat dry with a paper towel. Sprinkle the wrapper with 1 tsp of the sesame seeds. Line 2 mint leaves, 2 cilantro leaves, and 2 shrimp halves along the center, spacing them evenly. Soften a second wrapper and lay it over the first wrapper and fillings. Place 2 more shrimp halves, 2 pieces of cucumber, and mound some noodles along the center of the top wrapper. Tuck in the short ends of the wrapper and roll the summer roll gently but tightly, like a burrito.

5 Repeat to assemble the remaining summer rolls. Cut each roll in half on the diagonal, arrange, and serve with the remaining ponzu sauce.

# GRILLED COD

*Serves 4*

This dish reminds us of family summers at the beach, buying cod straight off the pier. Cooked simply on the grill with lemon, the freshness of the fish speaks for itself. Accompany with a green salad and celery root mash (page 144).

**Canola oil for brushing**

**4 tbsp (2 oz/60 g) unsalted butter, melted**

**1 tbsp fresh lemon juice**

**4 cod fillets, about 6 oz (185 g) each**

**Kosher salt and freshly ground pepper**

**2 lemons, quartered**

1 Build a hot fire in a charcoal grill, preheat a gas grill to high, or preheat a grill pan until smoking. Scrub the grill rack well and brush the rack or grill pan lightly with oil. In a small bowl, stir together the melted butter and lemon juice and set near the grill.

2 Brush the fillets on both sides with oil and season generously with salt and pepper.

3 Lay the fillets on the grill rack or in the pan directly at a 45-degree angle to the grill's grid and grill until the fish releases easily from the rack, 2–2½ minutes. Turn carefully and grill on the second side the same way until the fish is cooked through and flakes easily, 2–2½ minutes longer.

4 Transfer the fillets to a platter. Brush with the lemon butter and sprinkle with salt.

5 Arrange the lemon quarters on the grill or in the pan and grill until warmed and lightly grill marked, about 1 minute. Garnish the platter with the lemon quarters and serve.

# SHRIMP COCKTAIL

*Serves 4*

Surprise your family with this fresh take on the popular shrimp cocktail. All it requires is whipping up an easy homemade sauce. The more often you can make sauces and dressings from scratch, the better. Use ingredients like good olive oil and fresh lemon juice, and whatever you make will contain healthy nutrients. This recipe makes a light first course for 4 to 6 people.

**COCKTAIL SAUCE**

**1½ cups (10 oz/315 g) drained canned plum tomatoes, preferably San Marzano**

**¼ cup (2 fl oz/60 ml) chili sauce**

**2 tbsp prepared horseradish**

**1 tbsp olive oil**

**3 tbsp fresh lemon juice**

**1½ tsp sugar**

**½ tsp kosher salt**

**2 cups (16 fl oz/500 ml) vegetable stock or water**

**1 fresh thyme sprig**

**1 bay leaf**

**4 peppercorns**

**2 lemons, 1 halved, 1 cut into wedges**

**1 lb (500 g) jumbo shrimp, peeled and deveined**

1  To make the sauce, in a food processor, combine all the ingredients and process to a smooth purée. Transfer to a serving bowl or individual bowls, cover, and refrigerate until ready to serve.

2  In a large saucepan, combine the stock, thyme, bay leaf, peppercorns, and lemon halves and bring to a boil over medium-high heat. Reduce the heat to medium, add the shrimp, and poach just until cooked through, about 2 minutes. Drain immediately in a colander and place under cold running water to cool. Drain again thoroughly and pat dry with paper towels. Transfer to a glass serving bowl or individual plates, bowls, cocktail glasses, or parfait glasses and refrigerate, uncovered, until well chilled, about 1 hour.

3  Serve the shrimp cold with the cocktail sauce and lemon wedges.

# Tofu Pad Thai

*Serves 4–6*

An irresistible mix of sweet, tangy, and mildy spicy, this Thai-inspired noodle dish is a whole meal made in one pan. Once you get the hang of the stir-frying and timing, be creative and add any protein you like, or try it with whole-grain rice noodles. They'll provide lasting energy that helps curb afternoon sugar cravings.

¾ lb (375 g) dried rice noodles

3 tbsp tamarind paste

1 cup (8 fl oz/250 ml) boiling water

½ cup (4 fl oz/125 ml) reduced-sodium soy sauce

2 tbsp fish sauce

3 tbsp firmly packed golden brown sugar

1 tbsp tomato paste

¾ cup (6 fl oz/180 ml) canola oil

6 large eggs, beaten

1 lb (500 g) extra-firm tofu, cut into small cubes and patted dry

4 shallots, minced

6 cloves garlic, minced

4 green onions, white and tender green parts only, thinly sliced

1 cup (1 oz/30 g) bean sprouts

¼ cup (1½ oz/45 g) raw peanuts, coarsely chopped

1 lime, cut into wedges

1 Soak the noodles in a large bowl of very hot water (not boiling) to cover until softened, 5–8 minutes.

2 Meanwhile, put the tamarind paste in a small heatproof bowl, pour the boiling water over, and stir to dissolve. Transfer to a saucepan and add the soy sauce, fish sauce, brown sugar, and tomato paste. Place over medium heat and stir until the sugar dissolves, 1–2 minutes. Remove from the heat and set the sauce aside.

3 Heat ¼ cup (2 fl oz/60 ml) of the oil in a wok or large frying pan over medium heat. Add the eggs and cook until scrambled and fairly dry, 1–2 minutes. Transfer to a small bowl, let cool slightly, and shred with your fingers or chop into small pieces. Set aside.

4 Add the remaining ½ cup (4 fl oz/120 ml) oil to the pan and heat until the oil is just smoking. Add the tofu and toss and stir until golden brown on all sides, about 5 minutes. Using a slotted spoon, transfer to a plate and set aside.

5 Add the shallots and the garlic to the oil remaining in the pan and sauté until beginning to brown, 1–2 minutes. Add the tamarind sauce and bring to a boil. Add the noodles and toss and stir until tender and completely coated with the sauce and the liquid has been absorbed, about 3 minutes. Remove from the heat and add the tofu, eggs, green onions, and about half each of the bean sprouts and peanuts. Toss gently until the ingredients are well distributed and warmed through.

6 Mound the noodles on a serving platter or in individual bowls and scatter the remaining bean sprouts and peanuts over the top. Garnish with the lime wedges and serve right away.

# MARGHERITA PIZZA

*Serves 4*

What makes this classic pizza nearly everyone's favorite is the perfect balance of aromatic sweet basil, tomato sauce infused with fruity olive oil, a scattering of melted mozzarella, and a thin, crisp crust. It is utterly simple and delicious, packed with flavor that is both satisfying and familiar.

**Pizza Dough (page 183)**

**Cornmeal and all-purpose flour for dusting**

**1 cup (8 fl oz/250 ml) tomato sauce, homemade (page 184) or your favorite store-bought**

**2 large plum tomatoes, thinly sliced**

**2 cups (6 oz/185 g) shredded mozzarella cheese**

**2 tbsp finely shredded fresh basil**

**Kosher salt**

1 Make the dough and divide into 4 equal pieces. Shape each piece into a disk, and let rise for a second time as directed.

2 Preheat the oven to 400°F (200°C). Dust 2 large rimmed baking sheets with cornmeal.

3 On a lightly floured work surface, roll out 1 dough disk into an oval about 8 inches (20 cm) long, 4 inches (10 cm) wide, and ½ inch (12-mm) thick. Pinch around the edge to create a ½-inch (12-mm) rim, and place the oval on one-half of a cornmeal-dusted baking sheet. Spread about ¼ cup (2 fl oz/60 ml) of the tomato sauce evenly over the crust, leaving the rim uncovered. Arrange one-fourth of the tomato slices over the sauce. Sprinkle with about ½ cup (2 oz/60 g) of the mozzarella, ½ tbsp of the basil, and a pinch of salt. Repeat to assemble the second pizza, placing it on the other half of the baking sheet.

4 Bake until the dough is set and golden brown and the cheese has melted, 10–12 minutes. Meanwhile, assemble the remaining 2 pizzas on the second pan and slip them into the oven when the first batch is done. Cut all the pizzas into pieces and serve.

# Asparagus and Gruyère Pizza

*Serves 4*

Wondering how to get your kids excited about vegetables? This asparagus topping is the perfect solution. Experiment with other greenery, such as spinach or broccoli, fresh or frozen, to find out what your family likes best.

Pizza Dough (page 183)

Cornmeal and all-purpose flour for dusting

2 tsp olive oil

2 cloves garlic, coarsely chopped

1 lb (500 g) asparagus, woody ends discarded and spears thinly sliced on the diagonal

½ cup (2 oz/60 g) shredded mozzarella cheese

¼ cup (1 oz/30 g) shredded Gruyère cheese

Kosher salt

1 Make the dough and divide into 4 equal pieces. Shape each piece into a disk, and let rise for a second time as directed.

2 Preheat the oven to 400°F (200°C). Dust 2 large rimmed baking sheets with cornmeal.

3 In a small frying pan, heat the oil over medium heat. Add the garlic and sauté until softened and fragrant, 3–5 minutes. Strain the oil through a fine-mesh sieve into a heatproof bowl and set aside. Discard the garlic.

4 On a lightly floured work surface, roll out 1 dough disk into an oval about 8 inches (20 cm) long, 4 inches (10 cm) wide, and ½ inch (12 mm) thick. Pinch around the edge to create a ½-inch (12-mm) rim, and place the oval on one-half of a cornmeal-dusted baking sheet. Brush the dough lightly with the garlic oil. Arrange one-fourth of the asparagus slices evenly over the crust, leaving the rim uncovered. Sprinkle with one-fourth each of the mozzarella and the Gruyère, and a pinch of salt. Repeat to assemble the second pizza, placing it next to the first one on the other half of the baking sheet.

5 Bake until the dough is set and golden brown and the cheese has melted, 10–12 minutes. Meanwhile, assemble the remaining 2 pizzas on the second pan and slip them into the oven when the first batch is done. Cut all the pizzas into pieces and serve.

# BUTTERNUT SQUASH PIZZA

*Serves 4*

Make this fall favorite on a crisp, cool night using seasonal butternut squash, which will give you a boost of vitamin A and a dose of comforting energy. Two white cheeses and the deep orange flesh of the squash make for a beautiful pie.

**Pizza Dough (page 183)**

**1 small butternut squash, peeled, seeded, and cut lengthwise into wedges about 1 inch (2.5 cm) thick**

**Olive oil**

**Kosher salt**

**2 cloves garlic, coarsely chopped**

**Cornmeal and all-purpose flour for dusting**

**½ cup (2 oz/60 g) shredded mozzarella cheese**

**¼ cup (1 oz/30 g) shredded fontina cheese**

1 Make the dough and divide into 4 equal pieces. Shape each piece into a disk, and let rise for a second time as directed.

2 Preheat the oven to 400°F (200°C). Cut the squash wedges crosswise into slices about 1 inch (2.5 cm) thick. Transfer to a rimmed baking sheet. Drizzle with oil, sprinkle with salt, and toss to mix. Spread in an even layer and roast until tender-crisp, about 10 minutes. Set aside. Leave the oven on.

3 While the squash is roasting, in a small frying pan, heat 2 tsp oil over medium heat. Add the garlic and sauté until softened and fragrant, 3–5 minutes. Strain the oil through a fine-mesh sieve into a heatproof bowl and set aside. Discard the garlic.

4 Dust 2 large rimmed baking sheets with cornmeal. On a lightly floured work surface, roll out 1 dough disk into an oval about 8 inches (20 cm) long, 4 inches (10 cm) wide, and ½ inch (12 mm) thick. Pinch around the edge to create a ½-inch (12-mm) rim, and place the oval on one-half of a cornmeal-dusted baking sheet. Brush the dough lightly with the garlic oil. Arrange one-fourth of the squash slices evenly over the crust, leaving the rim uncovered. Sprinkle with one-fourth each of the mozzarella and the fontina, and a pinch of salt. Repeat to assemble the second pizza, placing it next to the first one on the other half of the baking sheet.

5 Bake until the dough is set and golden brown and the cheese has melted, 10–12 minutes. Meanwhile, assemble the remaining 2 pizzas on the second pan and slip them into the oven when the first batch is done. Cut all the pizzas into pieces and serve.

# Maple-Glazed Tofu Skewers

*Serves 4-6*

Tofu is a great source of protein and calcium, and a yummy vegetarian option for picky eaters. The leftover glaze will keep, tightly covered in the refrigerator, for up to 1 week. Drizzle it on soba noodles or brown rice with roasted vegetables for another quick weeknight vegetarian meal.

**GLAZE**

**2 cups (16 fl oz/500 ml) vegetable stock**

**⅓ cup (3½ fl oz/100 ml) pure maple syrup**

**⅓ cup (3 fl oz/90 ml) soy sauce**

**3 tbsp apple cider**

**1 tbsp fresh lemon juice**

**3 cloves garlic, smashed**

**3 tbsp cornstarch dissolved in 3 tbsp water**

**¼ cup (2 fl oz/60 ml) canola oil**

**2 lb (1 kg) extra-firm tofu, cut into ½-inch (12-mm) cubes and patted dry**

1 To make the glaze, in a saucepan, combine the stock, maple syrup, soy sauce, cider, lemon juice, and garlic and stir to combine. Place over medium-high heat and bring to a boil. Whisk in the cornstarch mixture and cook, whisking often, until the mixture begins to thicken, 3–4 minutes. Remove from the heat and set aside. The glaze will continue to thicken as it cools.

2 Heat the oil in a frying pan over medium-high heat. Working with 1 or 2 handfuls at a time to avoid sticking, drop the tofu cubes into the hot oil and fry, turning as needed, until browned on all sides, about 5 minutes total per batch. Using a slotted spoon, transfer the tofu to paper towels to drain.

3 When all of the tofu has been fried, thread the hot cubes onto 10 small wooden skewers, dividing them evenly. Arrange on a platter. Drizzle or brush some of the glaze over the skewers, and pour the remaining glaze into a small serving bowl. Serve the skewers and pass the extra glaze at the table for dipping.

# HOMEMADE RAVIOLI WITH SPINACH AND RICOTTA

*Serves 4–6*

This recipe is a good weekend family project. The dough (and the filled ravioli) freezes well; wrap tightly in plastic wrap or place in airtight freezer bags and freeze for up to 2 months. If you don't have time to make your own dough, use wonton wrappers. Cut them into circles using a cookie cutter or drinking glass, place the filling on one half of each circle, and fold in half, pinching the edges to seal.

**Fresh Pasta Dough (page 183)**

**1 cup (8 oz/250 g) fresh ricotta cheese**

**¼ cup (2 oz/60 g) thawed frozen chopped spinach, squeezed of excess liquid**

**¼ cup (1 oz/30 oz) grated Parmesan cheese, plus more for sprinkling**

**1 green onion, white and tender green parts only, thinly sliced**

**Kosher salt and freshly ground pepper**

**All-purpose flour for dusting**

**1 large egg, lightly beaten**

**3 cups (24 fl oz/750 ml) tomato sauce, homemade (page 184) or your favorite store-bought, warmed**

**Olive oil for drizzling**

1 Make the pasta dough and roll out as directed into 2 long sheets. Let rest for 15 minutes. Meanwhile, in a bowl, combine the ricotta, spinach, Parmesan, green onion, 2 tsp salt, and ½ tsp pepper and stir to mix well.

2 Cut 1 pasta sheet in half crosswise. Lay half of the sheet on a lightly floured work surface. Place mounds of the filling, each about 2 tsp, in a line lengthwise along the center of the sheet, starting about 1½ inches (4 cm) from one end, spacing the mounds about 3 inches (7.5 cm) apart, and stopping about 1½ inches (4 cm) from the opposite end. Brush all of the exposed pasta with the beaten egg, including between the mounds of filling. Lay the second half of the sheet over the first and line up the edges. Gently press the edges together to seal, pinching and smoothing all around the perimeter. Then press gently around each mound of filling to remove any air pockets and enclose the filling tightly. Repeat with the second pasta sheet and the remaining filling.

3 Use a square ravioli cutter, pastry wheel, or sharp knife to cut out 1½-inch (4-cm) square ravioli, first trimming the outer edges even. As you work, transfer the cut ravioli to a floured rimmed baking sheet.

4 Bring a large pot three-fourths full of salted water to a boil. Add the ravioli, stir gently once to prevent sticking, and cook until tender, 2–3 minutes. Using a slotted spoon, transfer the ravioli to a colander to drain. Transfer to a serving bowl and coat with the warm sauce. Drizzle with olive oil, sprinkle with Parmesan, and serve.

# Tomato-Mozzarella Lasagne

*Serves 6*

This classic is so easy to make at home. Using good-quality store-bought lasagne noodles saves time, as does keeping homemade tomato sauce (page 184) or your favorite jarred variety on hand. Simply assemble, bake, and eat. You can make a lasagne with as many layers as you like—4 to 8 layers generally work well. If you have extra sauce, freeze it for next time.

**Olive oil**

**Kosher salt and freshly ground pepper**

**10 wide (sometimes labeled "large") dried lasagne noodles**

**Nonstick cooking spray**

**2 cups (1 lb/500 g) fresh ricotta cheese**

**¼ cup (1 oz/30 g) grated Parmesan cheese, plus ⅓ cup (1¼ oz/35 g)**

**¼ cup (⅓ oz/10 g) fresh basil leaves, coarsely chopped**

**¼ cup (⅓ oz/10 g) fresh parsley leaves, coarsely chopped**

**2 tbsp dried oregano**

**4 cups (32 fl oz/1 l) tomato sauce, homemade (page 184) or your favorite store-bought**

**4 cups (1 lb/500 g) shredded mozzarella cheese**

1 Bring a large pot three-fourths full of salted water to a boil and add a splash of oil. Add the noodles, stir well to separate, and cook until al dente, about 4 minutes or according to the package directions. Drain and spread out on a lightly floured baking sheet or work surface.

2 Preheat the oven to 375°F (190°C). Lightly spray a standard loaf pan with cooking spray.

3 In a small bowl, combine the ricotta, the ¼ cup Parmesan, the basil, the parsley, the oregano, 2 tbsp salt, and ¼ pepper and stir to mix well. Set aside.

4 Spoon about ¼ cup (2 fl oz/60 ml) of the tomato sauce into the prepared pan and spread to cover the bottom. Spread about ¼ cup (2 oz/60 g) of the ricotta mixture in an even layer on 1 lasagne noodle and place in the pan on top of the tomato sauce. Spoon another ¼ cup of the sauce on top and add another noodle spread with ¼ cup of the ricotta mixture. Sprinkle this layer evenly with about ½ cup (2 oz/60 g) of the mozzarella. Repeat the entire process again 4 times (for 8 layers total), adding mozzarella every other layer. Top the final layer with the remaining tomato sauce and mozzarella, and the ⅓ cup (1¼ oz/35 g) Parmesan, in that order.

6 Cover tightly with aluminum foil and bake for 30 minutes. Uncover and continue to bake until the cheese begins to brown and the sauce is bubbling, about 15 minutes longer. Let cool for 15 minutes before serving, then cut into 1½-inch (4-cm) slices and serve.

# Meyer Lemon Gnocchi

Serves 4-6

Gnocchi is easy to prepare and fun to eat. Don't be afraid to make your own. It sounds hard, but it really isn't. Just allow some extra time to coax the piles of little dumplings into existence. There's no need to make each piece perfect, so long as they are plump and tender. Get the kids to help with rolling and indenting. The added step of pan searing the gnocchi, whether you use store-bought or homemade, creates an appealing and caramelized texture.

**2 packages (13 oz/410 g each) fresh gnocchi, or homemade (page 184)**

**Kosher salt**

**4 tbsp (2 oz/60 g) unsalted butter**

**Juice of 3 Meyer lemons**

**2 tbsp all-purpose flour**

**1 cup (8 fl oz/250 ml) chicken stock**

**1 tbsp finely chopped fresh flat-leaf parsley (optional)**

**Grated Parmesan cheese for serving**

1 Bring a large pot three-fourths full of lightly salted water to a boil over high heat. Add the gnocchi to the boiling water and cook until tender and cooked all the way through, about 4 minutes, or according to the package directions. Drain well and set aside.

2 In a large frying pan, melt the butter over medium-high heat and cook until foamy and hot. Working in batches as needed to avoid crowding, add the gnocchi, spread in an even layer, and sear until golden brown on the bottom, about 2 minutes. Transfer the gnocchi to a large serving bowl and return the pan to the stove top.

3 When all the gnocchi are in the bowl, pour the lemon juice into the pan and stir to scrape up any browned bits from the pan bottom. Reduce the heat to low and sprinkle the flour into the pan, whisking constantly to prevent lumps. Whisk in the chicken stock and 1 tsp salt and cook until the sauce has thickened and coats the back of a spoon, about 5 minutes. Stir in the parsley, if using, pour the sauce over the warm gnocchi, sprinkle with Parmesan, and serve.

# Sides

# SPINACH SQUARES

Serves 6–8

An SSC favorite, these delicious squares are nutrient packed: spinach is a good source of protein, calcium, fiber, iron, niacin, zinc, and vitamins A, C, K, and B6. Nevertheless, kids love these treats! Two cheeses complement the spinach perfectly, so the issue of "eating your vegetables" may never come up.

**2 tbsp unsalted butter, melted**

**3 large eggs**

**1 cup (8 fl oz/250 ml) whole milk**

**1 cup (5 oz/155 g) all-purpose flour**

**1 tsp baking powder**

**1 tsp kosher salt**

**1 lb (500 g) Cheddar cheese, shredded**

**1 lb (500 g) chopped frozen spinach, thawed and drained**

**¼ cup (1 oz/30 g) grated Parmesan cheese**

1 Preheat the oven to 375°F (190°C). Line a 9-by-13-inch (23-by-33-cm) rimmed baking sheet or baking dish with parchment paper. Pour the melted butter into the prepared pan and spread to coat evenly.

2 In a large bowl, beat the eggs until well blended. Whisk in the milk, flour, baking powder, and salt. Add the Cheddar and spinach and stir until combined. Pour the spinach mixture into the prepared pan and spread in an even layer. Sprinkle the Parmesan evenly over the top.

3 Bake until the top is lightly browned and the juices are bubbling, 30–40 minutes. Transfer to a wire rack and let cool until just warm to the touch. Cut into 2-inch (5-cm) squares and serve.

# BABY CANDIED CARROTS

Serves 4–6

Who needs a bowl of candies when you have these beauties at the table!
For the prettiest dish, check out your local farmers' market for a first-rate
selection of baby carrots in a variety of colors: creamy white, bright orange,
deep purple, sunshine yellow. If baby carrots aren't available, try this same
method with any root vegetable that looks good at the market.

**1 lb (500 g) baby
carrots, preferably
a variety of colors**

**1 tbsp canola oil**

**1 tbsp honey**

**½ tsp salt**

1 Peel the carrots and trim down the leafy tops but leave them whole.

2 In a nonstick frying pan, heat the oil over medium heat. Add the
carrots and cook, shaking the pan often to ensure they cook evenly,
until they begin to soften, about 5 minutes. Drizzle the honey over
the carrots, toss to coat evenly, and then continue to cook until just
tender, 2–3 minutes longer.

3 Season with the salt, transfer to a platter, and serve.

# POLENTA FRIES WITH KETCHUP

*Makes about 60 fries*

This Italian-inspired finger food is a great substitute for French fries, in part because it looks just like them! But you don't need to carry the deception too far. Kids like the tender texture and full, sweet corn flavor of polenta, especially when it can be dipped in tasty homemade ketchup. This recipe scores a high health grade thanks to baking instead of frying. Cornmeal is also an excellent alternative for anyone who can't eat gluten.

**Nonstick cooking spray**

**2 qt (2 l) water**

**2¼ cups (1 lb/500 g) instant polenta**

**1 cup (8 fl oz/250 ml) whole milk**

**½ cup (2 oz/60 g) grated Parmesan cheese**

**3 tbsp unsalted butter, at room temperature**

**Kosher salt and freshly ground pepper**

**Ketchup, homemade (page 185) or your favorite store-bought, for serving**

**1** Spray a large rimmed baking sheet with cooking spray and line the pan with parchment paper.

**2** In a heavy-bottomed saucepan, bring the water to a boil over high heat. Reduce the heat to a simmer and slowly add the polenta while whisking constantly. Cook, continuing to whisk, until the polenta has thickened, about 3 minutes. Remove from the heat. Add the milk, Parmesan, butter, 1 tbsp salt, and ½ tsp pepper and stir with a wooden spoon until thoroughly incorporated and the polenta is smooth.

**3** Pour the polenta into the center of the prepared baking sheet. Using a rubber spatula, spread it toward one end of the pan, pushing it into the corners and then to the edges, covering about two-thirds of the pan in an even layer. Spray a second piece of parchment with cooking spray and gently press the coated side onto the polenta to level and smooth the surface. Let cool at room temperature until set, about 1 hour.

**4** Preheat the oven to 400°F (200°C). Remove the top sheet of parchment and cut the polenta into strips about ½ inch (12 mm) wide and 4 inches (10 cm) long. Using a spatula, transfer the strips to a clean rimmed baking sheet, spacing them about ½ inch (12 mm) apart. Spray the fries lightly with cooking spray and sprinkle with salt.

**5** Bake until the fries have developed a crust and the edges are golden, about 30 minutes. Let cool slightly, then serve with the ketchup.

# Arancini

Serves 4–6

Transport your family with this tempting Italian street food. Traditionally made with Arborio rice, these irresistible rice balls can be stuffed with whatever you please—cheese, ham—to make dinner more convenient. The recipe probably won't require any shopping as you likely already have everything in your pantry.

1 tbsp olive oil, plus more for frying

½ yellow onion, minced

½ cup (3½ oz/105 g) short- or long-grain brown rice

2 cups (16 fl oz/500 ml) chicken or vegetable stock, plus more if needed

½ cup (2 oz/60 g) grated Parmesan cheese

½ cup (½ oz/15 g) panko bread crumbs

1 large egg white, beaten

8 oz (250 g) low-moisture mozzarella or other semifirm cheese such as fontina, cut into ¼-inch (6-mm) cubes

Kosher salt

1 Heat the oil in a saucepan over medium heat. Add the onion and sauté until translucent, about 5 minutes. Add the rice and stir to coat with the oil. Add the 2 cups stock, raise the heat to high, and bring to a boil. Reduce the heat to low, cover tightly, and simmer until all the liquid is absorbed, about 20 minutes. The rice needs to be a bit overcooked and sticky. Add more stock, a little at a time, if needed.

2 When the rice has finished cooking, remove from the heat and stir in the Parmesan and ¼ cup (¼ oz/7 g) of the bread crumbs. Spread the mixture on a baking sheet and let cool completely. When cooled, add the egg white and toss and stir to mix well.

3 Using dampened hands, scoop up about 2 tbsp of the rice mixture and shape it around a cheese cube to a make ball about 2 inches (5 cm) in diameter. Make sure the cheese is fully enclosed in the rice. Repeat to form 9 more balls.

4 Spread the remaining ¼ cup of bread crumbs on a shallow plate and coat each rice ball thoroughly with the crumbs, shaking off any excess.

5 Pour oil to a depth of ½ inch (12 mm) into a nonstick frying pan and heat until hot but not smoking. Working in batches as needed to avoid crowding, add the rice balls and fry, turning as needed, until browned on all sides and crisp, about 10 minutes. Using a slotted spoon, transfer to paper towels to drain and sprinkle with salt while still hot. Transfer to the prepared baking sheet to drain and keep warm in the oven. Repeat to cook the remaining rice balls, adding a little more oil to the pan, if needed.

6 When all of the arancini are cooked, arrange them on a platter or individual plates and serve.

# ROASTED BABY POTATOES

Serves 6–8

Roasting potatoes is a great heart-healthy alternative to frying potatoes, and we guarantee that you and your kids will hardly notice the difference. This recipe is a proverbial snap. Use any leftovers for making hash browns for breakfast, sautéing them with bell peppers and onions for an easy side, or transforming them into a yummy potato salad by adding a bit of mayonnaise and lemon juice.

**2 lb (1 kg) baby potatoes, preferably a variety of colors**

**2 tsp salt**

**1 tbsp olive oil**

**1 tsp freshly ground pepper**

1 Place the potatoes in a saucepan, add water to cover, and bring to a boil over medium-high heat. Stir in 1 tsp of the salt, reduce the heat to low, and simmer, uncovered, until the potatoes are just tender when pierced with a fork, 12–20 minutes, depending on their size.

2 Drain the potatoes and arrange in a single layer on a rimmed baking sheet. Let stand until dry, about 5 minutes. Meanwhile, preheat the oven to 400°F (200°C).

3 Transfer the dry potatoes to a bowl, drizzle with the oil, and stir and toss to coat evenly. Arrange the potatoes in a single layer on the baking sheet. Roast until golden on the top side, about 10 minutes. Turn the potatoes and continue to roast until golden on the second side, about 10 minutes longer.

4 Transfer the potatoes to a serving dish, season with the remaining 1 tsp salt and the pepper, toss to coat evenly, and serve.

# PAN-SEARED BROCCOLI

*Serves 4–6*

Here is a tasty, simple alternative to steamed broccoli—and it comes together just as quickly. Blanching renders the broccoli tender but bright green, searing gives it an irresistible crispy quality, and the lemon juice brings out its natural flavor. You can also add these florets to freshly steamed rice or to a salad.

**Kosher salt**

**1 head broccoli, cut into florets**

**2 tbsp olive oil**

**1 lemon, halved**

**Freshly ground pepper**

1 Have ready a large bowl of ice water. Bring a large saucepan three-fourths full of lightly salted water to a boil over high heat. Add the broccoli and blanch for 30 seconds, but no longer—the broccoli should remain bright green and crunchy. Drain the florets and immediately plunge into the ice water to stop the cooking. Let stand until the broccoli is cool to the touch. Drain well.

2 Heat the oil in a large frying pan over medium-high heat. When the oil begins to ripple and shimmer, add the broccoli florets and toss to coat with the oil. Sear the florets quickly on one side until they have some golden brown spots and begin to caramelize, about 30 seconds. Toss again and sear quickly on the second side, about 30 seconds longer, then remove from the heat.

3 Squeeze the lemon halves over the broccoli, season with 1 tsp salt and ½ tsp pepper, and toss again to mix. Transfer to a platter, and serve.

# SCALLOPED POTATOES

*Serves 4–6*

This comforting dish of tender potatoes and bubbling cheese sauce is always a crowd-pleaser. Recruit family members to help assemble the elements. Each person can be responsible for preparing one item—shredding the cheese, cubing the butter, slicing the potatoes—and then everyone can feel proud of the delicious results when they sit down at the table for dinner together.

**3 tbsp cold unsalted butter, cut into tiny cubes, plus more for greasing**

**¾ cup (6 fl oz/180 ml) heavy cream**

**¼ cup (2 fl oz/60 ml) whole milk**

**1 large egg, beaten**

**½ tsp freshly grated nutmeg**

**2 tsp kosher salt**

**1 tsp freshly ground pepper**

**2 lb (1 kg) Yukon gold potatoes, peeled**

**½ lb (250 g) Gruyère cheese, shredded**

1 Preheat the oven to 400°F (200°C). Grease a large 9- or 10-inch (23- or 25-cm) square or round baking dish with butter.

2 In a large bowl, whisk together the cream, milk, egg, nutmeg, salt, and pepper. Slice the potatoes thinly, no more than about ⅛ inch (3 mm) thick, preferably on a mandoline. The slices should be translucent. Place the potatoes in the cream mixture and toss gently to coat. (This will prevent the potatoes from browning.)

3 Line the bottom of the prepared dish with about one-fifth of the potatoes. Dot the layer with a generous 2 tsp of the butter and sprinkle with about ⅓ cup (1⅓ oz/40 g) of the cheese. Repeat to make 3 more layers, then finish with the last of the potatoes. Press the assembled layers down with the back of a spatula to pack them. Pour the cream mixture remaining in the bowl over the potatoes, stopping when it is just visible around the edges of the dish. Sprinkle the remaining cheese evenly over the top.

4 Cover the dish with aluminum foil and bake until the potatoes are cooked through and tender with a tiny bit of resistance when pierced with a fork, about 25 minutes. Remove the foil and continue to bake until the top is golden brown and the juices are bubbling, 10–15 minutes longer. Let cool slightly, then serve.

# Mac-n-Cheese Muffins

*Makes 12 muffins*

This is a fun, unexpected, and absolutely fabulous new way to enjoy an old favorite. The satisfying, cheesy cupcakes-for-dinner are cute and just as easy to make as they are to eat. We suggest using organic cheese and milk, if available.

½ cup (4 oz/125 g) unsalted butter, plus more for greasing

¼ cup (1½ oz/45 g) all-purpose flour, plus more for dusting

1 lb (500 g) elbow macaroni

5 cups (40 fl oz/1.25 l) whole milk

1½ lb (750 g) sharp Cheddar cheese, shredded

½ cup (2 oz/60 g) grated Parmesan cheese

1 tsp kosher salt

½ tsp freshly ground pepper

**TOPPING**

4 tbsp (2 oz/60 g) unsalted butter, melted

½ cup (½ oz/15 g) panko bread crumbs

¼ cup (1 oz/30 g) grated Parmesan cheese

1 Preheat the oven to 375°F (190°C). Grease a standard 12-cup muffin pan with butter, then dust with flour, tapping out the excess.

2 Bring a saucepan three-fourths full of salted water to a boil over high heat. Add the macaroni, stir once, and return to a boil. Cook until just shy of al dente, 6–7 minutes. Drain, reserving 1 cup (8 fl oz/250 ml) of the cooking water. Set the macaroni and reserved cooking water aside.

3 In a heavy-bottomed saucepan, melt the butter over medium-low heat. Stir in the flour and cook, stirring constantly, until the mixture just starts to darken, about 3 minutes. Whisking constantly, slowly add the milk, raise the heat, and bring the sauce to a boil. Reduce the heat to maintain a simmer and cook, stirring occasionally, until the sauce begins to thicken, 3–5 minutes longer.

4 Add the cheeses, salt, and pepper to the sauce and stir until all the cheese is melted and the sauce is smooth. Remove from the heat. Add the macaroni and stir to coat thoroughly. Cover to keep warm.

5 To make the topping, in a small bowl, stir together the butter, bread crumbs, and Parmesan until well mixed.

6 Fill each prepared muffin cup to the rim with the macaroni mixture. Sprinkle the muffins with the topping, dividing it evenly. Bake until the tops are golden brown and the sauce is bubbling, 15–20 minutes. Transfer to a wire rack and let cool completely in the pan, then refrigerate the muffins, still in the pan, for at least 2 hours or up to 24 hours so they will hold their shape.

7 Unmold the muffins using a small, sharp knife. Rewarm in a 350°F (180°C) oven for about 5 minutes, and serve.

# Farro with Caramelized Root Vegetables

*Serves 4–6*

Farro, a hearty, healthy, and highly prized Italian grain, fits comfortably into menus year-round. In fall, we like it tossed with roasted root vegetables. This dish is sweet and savory and loses nothing when served at room temperature, making it a great option for the lunch box or for the salad plate.

1⅓ cups (8 oz/250 g) pearled farro

1¾ cups (14 fl oz/430 ml) vegetable or chicken stock

Kosher salt

2 tbsp olive oil

1 small yellow onion, cut into ¼-inch (6-mm) dice

1 turnip, peeled and cut into ¼-inch (6-mm) dice

2 carrots, peeled and cut into ¼-inch (6-mm) dice

2 parsnips, peeled and cut into ¼-inch (6-mm) dice

1 tbsp honey

Freshly ground pepper

1 Heat a heavy-bottomed saucepan over medium-high heat and add the farro. Using a wooden spoon, stir often until lightly toasted and aromatic, about 3 minutes. Add the stock and 2 tsp salt and bring to a boil. Reduce the heat to low, cover, and simmer until all the stock is absorbed and the farro is tender but with a bit of a bite remaining at the center, 12–15 minutes. Transfer to a large serving bowl and set aside to cool.

2 While the farro is cooling, heat the oil in a large frying pan over medium-low heat. Add all of the vegetables and toss to coat with the oil. Sauté the vegetables until they start to release their liquid, about 5 minutes. Raise the heat to medium-high and cook until they are golden and have begun to caramelize, 10–15 minutes longer. Stir in the honey and season with salt and pepper.

3 Add the vegetables to the bowl with the farro and toss to combine. Taste and adjust the seasoning. Serve warm or at room temperature.

# Sweet Potato Pancakes

*Makes about 16 pancakes*

Vibrantly orange sweet potatoes are high in vitamins and fiber, making them a healthful addition to any menu. Nowadays, cooks typically cut them into batons and make sweet potato fries. But we like to make these pancakes, which get wonderfully crispy in less oil than you would use if deep-frying. Alternatively, you could make bite-sized pancakes and top them with crème fraîche and chopped green onions for a tasty, eye-catching hors d'oeuvre.

1 lb (500 g) orange-fleshed sweet potatoes

¼ cup (¾ oz/20 g) thinly sliced green onions, white and tender green parts only

1 large egg, beaten

¼ cup (1½ oz/45 g) all-purpose flour

Kosher salt

Freshly ground pepper

Canola oil

1 Peel the sweet potatoes. Using the largest holes of a box grater-shredder, shred them and place in a large bowl. Add the green onions, egg, flour, 2 tsp salt, and ¾ tsp pepper and, using your hands or a wooden spoon, mix together well.

2 Line a rimmed baking sheet with paper towels. Pour oil to a depth of ¼ inch (6 mm) into a large nonstick frying pan and heat over medium-high heat until hot and shimmering but not smoking.

3 Preheat the oven to 200°F (95°C). Using a 2-tbsp scoop, drop rounds of the sweet potato mixture into the hot oil. Do not crowd the pan. Using the back of the scoop, gently flatten each round slightly; the pancakes should be about 2 inches (5 cm) in diameter. Fry, turning once, until golden brown and crispy, 2–3 minutes per side. Transfer to the prepared baking sheet to drain and keep warm in the oven. Repeat to cook the remaining pancakes, adding a little more oil to the pan, if needed.

4 When all of the pancakes are ready, arrange them on a platter, sprinkle generously with salt, and serve.

# CORN PANCAKES

*Makes about 12 pancakes*

Make these savory pancakes in the summer months, when ears of sweet corn are filling market bins. If you still crave them out of season, good-quality frozen corn will do. For a fabulous party snack, make bite-sized pancakes and top with a dollop of sour cream and a slice of smoked salmon—or, for a special occasion, crème fraîche, caviar, and fresh dill.

**5 ears corn, husks and silk removed, or 2 cups (12 oz/375 g) thawed frozen corn**

**¾ cup (6 fl oz/180 ml) whole milk**

**3 large eggs, beaten**

**2 tbsp unsalted butter, melted and cooled slightly**

**1 cup (7 oz/220 g) instant polenta or coarse-grind yellow cornmeal**

**1 tbsp all-purpose flour**

**1 tbsp grated Parmesan cheese**

**1 tsp kosher salt**

**1 tsp freshly ground pepper**

**1 tbsp canola oil, or as needed**

1 If using fresh corn, pour water to a depth of 1 inch (2.5 cm) into a large saucepan and bring to a boil. Place a steamer basket in the pan, add the corn to the basket, cover, and steam just until tender, about 8 minutes. Using tongs, transfer the corn to a plate and let cool. Using a large, sharp knife, cut the kernels from the cobs.

2 Place the corn in a food processor and pulse until coarsely chopped and a little wet. Transfer to a large bowl. Add the milk, eggs, and butter and stir until well blended. In a small bowl, whisk together the polenta, flour, Parmesan, salt, and pepper. Add the dry ingredients to the wet ingredients and stir just until combined.

3 Preheat the oven to 200°F (95°C). In a large nonstick frying pan, heat the oil over medium heat. To form each pancake, fill a ½-cup (4–fl oz/125-ml) ladle with the batter and drop it into the pan. Do not crowd the pan. Cook on the first side until the edges are golden, about 3 minutes, then turn the pancakes and cook on the second side until golden, about 3 minutes longer. Transfer to a rimmed baking sheet and keep warm in the oven. Repeat to cook the remaining pancakes, adding a little more oil to the pan, if needed.

4 When all of the pancakes are ready, arrange them on a platter or individual plates and serve.

# ZUCCHINI FRITTERS

*Makes about 12 fritters*

Turning squash into these crispy, golden nuggets is another tasty way to take advantage of summertime's vegetable bounty. We like these fritters as snacks or sides. Be sure to let the shredded zucchini drain thoroughly as well as squeezing out any excess moisture; this ensures that the fritters will have that delectable crunch. Zucchini promotes energy and good digestion.

**2 lb (1 kg) zucchini**

**Kosher salt**

**1 large egg, beaten**

**½ cup (½ oz/15 g) panko bread crumbs**

**¼ cup (1½ oz/45 g) all-purpose flour**

**2 shallots, minced**

**2 tbsp grated lemon zest**

**Freshly ground pepper**

**Canola oil for frying**

1 Trim the ends of the zucchini. Using the large holes of a box grater-shredder, shred the zucchini. Transfer to a colander and toss with a large pinch of salt. Place the colander over a large bowl and let the zucchini drain for about 30 minutes.

2 Wrap the zucchini in a clean kitchen towel and squeeze gently to remove excess water. Transfer to a bowl. Add the egg, bread crumbs, flour, shallots, lemon zest, 1 tsp salt, and ½ tsp pepper and, using your hands, toss gently until well mixed.

3 Line a rimmed baking sheet with paper towels. Pour oil to a depth of ¼ inch (6 mm) into a large nonstick frying pan and heat over medium-high heat until hot and shimmering but not smoking.

4 Preheat the oven to 200°F (95°C). Using a 2-tbsp scoop, drop rounds of the zucchini mixture into the hot oil. Do not crowd the pan. Using the back of the scoop, gently flatten each round slightly; the fritters should be about 2 inch (5 cm) in diameter. Fry, turning once, until golden brown and crispy, about 3 minutes per side. Transfer to the prepared baking sheet to drain and keep warm in the oven. Repeat to cook the remaining fritters, adding a little more oil to the pan, if needed.

5 When all of the fritters are ready, arrange them on a platter, sprinkle with salt, and serve.

# CELERY ROOT
# MASHED POTATOES

Serves 4-6

This adaptation of mashed potatoes has just as much flavor as the classic but is even better for you with the addition of celery root. The texture of celery root (also know as celeriac) is similar to that of potato, both raw and cooked. When prepared like potatoes with butter and cream, it has an even earthier, more comforting flavor and gets higher marks for potassium.

**2 cups (14 oz/440 g) peeled and thinly sliced Yukon gold potatoes (2 or 3 large potatoes)**

**2 cups (14 oz/440 g) peeled and thinly sliced celery root (2 medium heads)**

**2 tbsp unsalted butter**

**¼ cup (2 fl oz/60 ml) heavy cream, plus more if needed**

**1½ tsp kosher salt**

1 Place the potatoes and celery root in separate saucepans and add water to both pans to cover by 1 inch (2.5 cm). Bring both pans to a boil over medium-high heat, then reduce the heat to low and simmer, uncovered, until the vegetables are very tender, 10–15 minutes for the potatoes and 15–20 minutes for the celery root.

2 Drain both pans into a large colander placed in the sink. Return one of the warm pots to the stove top and add the butter, cream, and salt. Pass the celery root and potatoes through a food mill or ricer into the pot. Stir well to incorporate the butter and milk, adding a little bit more cream if the mash seems dry.

3 Taste and adjust the seasoning, then transfer to a bowl and serve.

# MINI TWICE-BAKED POTATOES

*Makes 24 pieces; serves 4–6*

A star tip in your pastry bag is the key to making these little packages pretty. Chilling the filling briefly will make piping easier and help the peaks maintain their fluted pattern. Any small round potato will do. Visit your farmers' market for the freshest choices. For the best flavor and good health, we recommend using organic milk and sour cream. These make fantastic party fare.

**Canola oil for greasing**

**24 baby Yukon gold potatoes, about 1 inch (2.5 cm) in diameter (about 3½ lb/1.75 kg total weight)**

**½ cup (4 oz/125 g) sour cream**

**¼ cup (2 fl oz/60 ml) whole milk**

**¼ cup (⅓ oz/10 g) minced fresh chives, plus 1-inch (2.5-cm) lengths for garnish**

**2 tsp kosher salt**

**1 tsp freshly ground pepper**

1 Preheat the oven to 450°F (230°C). Lightly grease a rimmed baking sheet with oil.

2 Arrange the potatoes in a single layer on the prepared baking sheet and bake until tender when pierced with a fork and the skin has begun to wrinkle and pull away from the flesh, 15–20 minutes. Remove from the oven and let stand until cool enough to handle. Leave the oven on.

3 When cooled, cut 12 of the potatoes in half lengthwise. Using a melon baller, cut out a scoop from the center of each potato half, leaving a wall of flesh about ¼ inch (6 mm) thick. Transfer the scooped flesh to a food mill or ricer, and return the hollowed-out potato halves, hollow side up, to the baking sheet. Set the baking sheet aside. Pass the potato flesh through the mill or ricer into a large bowl.

4 Peel the remaining 12 potatoes, then pass them through the mill or ricer into the bowl. Add the sour cream, milk, minced chives, salt, and pepper and stir until smooth. Refrigerate the filling for 5–10 minutes. Transfer the filling to a pastry bag fitted with a large star tip. (Alternatively, scoop the filling into a large zippered plastic bag and snip off one corner of the bag to make a ½-inch/12-mm opening.) Pipe the filling into the hollowed-out potato halves, mounding it about 1 inch (2.5 cm) high. The filling will shrink as it bakes.

5 Bake the filled potatoes until the tops are lightly browned, 5–7 minutes. Remove from the oven and let cool slightly. Garnish each potato half with a chive piece or two and serve.

# SESAME SUGAR SNAP PEAS

Serves 4–6

A perfect summer treat, these peas are sweet, crisp, and—bonus!—salty.
This side dish can also be eaten out of hand, making it a good choice for the
beach or a picnic, where little fingers can hold the sugar snaps with ease.
The dressing is bright and versatile. Use it on your next tossed green salad.

**Kosher salt**

**2 lb (1 kg) sugar snap
peas, trimmed and
any strings removed**

**3 tbsp seasoned
rice vinegar**

**1 tbsp soy sauce**

**1 tbsp Asian sesame oil**

**1 tbsp firmly packed
golden brown sugar**

**Freshly ground pepper**

**1 tbsp black sesame seeds**

1 Have ready a large bowl of ice water. Bring a large saucepan three-fourths full of lightly salted water to a boil over high heat. Add the peas and blanch for 30 seconds, but no longer. You want them to be bright green and crunchy. Drain the peas and immediately plunge them into the ice water to stop the cooking. Let stand until cool to the touch, then drain well and transfer to a serving bowl.

2 In a small bowl, whisk together the vinegar, soy sauce, sesame oil, brown sugar, 1 tsp salt, and ½ tsp pepper until well blended. Pour the dressing over the peas and toss to coat. Taste and adjust the seasoning. Sprinkle with the sesame seeds and serve.

# ROASTED ASPARAGUS

*Serves 4–6*

Fresh springtime asparagus is a great go-to vegetable: elegant, simple to prepare, versatile, and delicious. Any leftovers are just as good cold, or try chopping them and adding them to a salad, scrambled eggs, or an omelet.

**1 lb (500 g) slender asparagus spears**

**2 tbsp olive oil**

**1 tsp kosher salt**

**½ tsp freshly ground pepper**

1 Preheat the oven to 400°F (200°C).

2 Cut off and discard the woody end from each asparagus spear. Pile the asparagus on a rimmed baking sheet. Drizzle with the oil and sprinkle with the salt and pepper. Using your hands, rub the spears to coat thoroughly with the oil and seasonings, then spread in a single layer on the pan.

3 Roast until tender but still bright green, 8–10 minutes. Transfer to a platter and serve.

# HARICOTS VERTS WITH LEMON

Serves 4–6

Easy, easy, easy does it. The key to perfectly prepared and nutritious vegetables is to cook them so they are tender but still crisp. An ice-water bath stops the cooking, which otherwise can easily continue to a point of mush, and lemon juice brings out the flavor. If you cannot find long, skinny French haricots verts, use regular green beans or even snap peas.

**Kosher salt**

**2 lb (1 kg) haricots verts or other slender green beans, trimmed and any strings removed**

**3 tbsp unsalted butter**

**1 lemon, halved**

1  Have ready a large bowl of ice water. Bring a large saucepan three-fourths full of lightly salted water to a boil over high heat. Add the beans and blanch for 30 seconds, but no longer. You want them to be bright green and crunchy. Drain the beans and immediately plunge them into the ice water to stop the cooking. Let stand until cool to the touch, then drain well.

2  Melt the butter in a large frying pan over medium-low heat. When the butter begins to foam, add the beans and toss to coat. Toss and stir until the beans are tender but still have a bit of crunch, about 3 minutes, then remove from the heat.

3  Squeeze the lemon halves over the beans, sprinkle with salt, and toss again to mix. Transfer to a serving bowl or platter and serve.

# SPAGHETTI SQUASH WITH TOMATO SAUCE

Serves 4-6

Spaghetti squash is a gift: it magically shreds into long, noodlelike strands when cooked, making it a delicious and nutritious substitute for pasta. It's fun to eat and is a good way to add vitamins, nutrients, and fiber to your diet. Squash is also high in potassium, which helps lower blood pressure.

**2 lb (1 kg) spaghetti squash**

**1 tbsp olive oil, plus more for drizzling**

**Kosher salt and freshly ground pepper**

**3 cups (24 fl oz/750 ml) tomato sauce, homemade (page 184) or your favorite store-bought, warmed**

1 Preheat the oven to 400°F (200°C).

2 Cut the squash in half lengthwise and scoop out the seeds. Brush the flesh with the 1 tbsp oil and sprinkle with 2 tsp salt and ½ tsp pepper. Place the squash halves, cut side down, on a rimmed baking sheet.

3 Roast until tender and easily pierced with a fork, 45–60 minutes. Remove from the oven and set aside until cool enough to handle. Using a fork, gently scrape the squash in lengthwise strokes. The flesh will naturally come away in long strands.

4 Pour half of the warm sauce into a large bowl. Add the squash and toss gently to coat with the sauce. Drizzle with a little oil, season with salt and pepper, and serve. Pass the remaining sauce at the table.

# FARRO WITH FRESH CORN AND SUGAR SNAP PEAS

Serves 4–6

Here is our summertime recipe for a farro side dish that can double as a salad. Be careful not to overcook the peas and corn or their bright flavors will be lost. Pack this dish for a picnic, or serve it as a side with poultry, steak, or fish.

2¼ cups (1 lb/500 g) pearled farro

4 cups (32 fl oz/1 l) vegetable stock

Kosher salt

2 tbsp olive oil

1 yellow onion, finely chopped

1 lb (500 g) sugar snap peas, cut on the diagonal into ¼-inch (6-mm) pieces

Kernels from 4 ears of fresh corn or 2 cups (12 oz/375 g) thawed frozen corn

¾ cup (6 fl oz/180 ml) cider vinegar

Freshly ground pepper

1 Heat a heavy-bottomed saucepan over medium-high heat and add the farro. Using a wooden spoon, stir often until lightly toasted and aromatic, about 3 minutes. Add the stock and 1 tbsp salt and bring to a boil. Reduce the heat to low, cover, and simmer until all the stock is absorbed and the farro is tender but with a bit of a bite remaining at the center, 12–15 minutes. Transfer to a large serving bowl and set aside to cool.

2 While the farro is cooling, heat the oil in a large frying pan over medium-low heat. Add the onion and sauté until softened and translucent, about 10 minutes. Add the peas and corn and sauté until just tender, about 5 minutes longer.

3 Add the vegetables to the farro, drizzle with the vinegar, and toss to mix well. Taste and adjust the seasoning with salt and pepper. Serve warm or at room temperature.

# Jasmine Rice with Dried Fruit and Pine Nuts

*Serves 4*

You can make this quick-to-assemble rice dish up to 1 day in advance and either rewarm it gently just before serving, or serve it at room temperature. It has a fantastic salty-sweet contrast that goes perfectly with dishes like our chicken tikka masala (page 67) or Miso Cod (page 94). If you cannot find jasmine rice, regular long-grain white rice can be substituted.

½ cup (2½ oz/75 g)
**pine nuts**

**2 tbsp olive oil**

**1 yellow onion,
finely chopped**

**1½ cups (10½ oz/330 g)
jasmine rice**

**3 cups (24 fl oz/750 ml)
vegetable stock or water,
or a combination**

**1 tsp kosher salt**

⅓ cup (2 oz/60 g)
**chopped dried apricots**

⅓ cup (2 oz/60 g)
**dried cranberries**

1  In a small, dry frying pan, toast the pine nuts over medium heat, stirring constantly, until fragrant and lightly browned, about 5 minutes. Watch closely as the nuts can scorch easily. Transfer immediately to a plate and let cool.

2  In a nonstick saucepan, heat 1 tbsp of the oil over medium heat. Add the onion and sauté until softened, 5–7 minutes. Add the rice and stir to coat the grains with the oil. Add the stock and salt and stir to mix. Bring to a simmer and cook, covered, until all of the liquid has been absorbed, about 15 minutes. Remove from the heat and let cool slightly.

3  Transfer the rice to a large serving bowl and fluff the grains with a fork. Add the apricots, cranberries, toasted pine nuts, and the remaining 1 tbsp oil, stir to mix well, and serve.

# Ponzu Bok Choy

Serves 4–6

Bok choy, with its appealing crunch and pleasantly mild, leafy green tops, converts many picky eaters who "don't like vegetables" or who are hesitant about Asian cuisine. Make this easy side dish and watch people ask for seconds. The cooking method and the light, salty, savory sauce can also be used with other sturdy greens, such as kale, chard, or even broccoli.

**2 lb (1 kg) baby bok choy, preferably Shanghai**

**¼ cup (2 fl oz/60 ml) Asian sesame oil**

**½ cup (4 fl oz/125 ml) ponzu sauce, store-bought or a mixture of ⅓ cup (3 fl oz/80 ml) soy sauce with the juice of 1 lemon**

1 Trim the base of the bok choy, then cut each head in half lengthwise, or into quarters if large.

2 Heat the sesame oil in a large frying pan over medium-high heat until it ripples but is not smoking. Add the bok choy and sear until the leaves have wilted slightly and the stems are tender, 3–4 minutes.

3 To finish, pour the ponzu sauce around the pan and toss and stir just until the bok choy is lightly glazed with the sauce, about 1 minute. Transfer to a platter and serve.

# Quinoa Cakes

*Makes about 10 cakes*

An ancient grain that is now wildly popular, quinoa has tender, barleylike texture and earthy-nutty flavor. A complete protein, it is also versatile and easy to cook, making it a convenient choice for incorporating nutrition into your menus. These little cheese-laced cakes are an appealing starter or snack. Susie's Tip: Cook quinoa until al dente—tender but with a slight bite in the center of the grain.

1¾ cups (14 oz/440 g) quinoa

1⅓ cups (11 fl oz/345 ml) vegetable stock or water

1 cup (5 oz/155 g) all-purpose flour

5 oz (155 g) low-moisture mozzarella cheese, cut into ¼-inch (6-mm) dice

¼ cup (1 oz/30 g) grated Parmesan cheese

Kosher salt and freshly ground pepper

4 green onions, white and tender green parts only, thinly sliced

1 large egg

2 large egg yolks

Canola oil for frying

1 Heat a heavy-bottomed saucepan over medium-high heat and add the quinoa. Using a wooden spoon, stir constantly until lightly toasted and aromatic, about 5 minutes. Pour in the stock and bring to a boil. Reduce the heat to medium-low, cover, and simmer until the water has been absorbed and the quinoa is tender but with a bit of a bite remaining at the center, 10–12 minutes. Remove from the heat and let cool completely.

2 Add the flour, cheeses, 1 tsp salt, and ¼ tsp pepper to the cooled quinoa and toss gently to mix, using your hands or a rubber spatula. Stir in the green onions, whole egg, and egg yolks until the mixture comes together and resembles a soft dough.

3 Shape the mixture into 10 cakes each about 2 inches (5 cm) in diameter and 1½ inches (4 cm) thick, arranging them on a baking sheet as you work. Use a ⅓-cup (3–fl oz/80-ml) measuring cup as a guide, if you like. Refrigerate for about 10 minutes to set.

4 Preheat the oven to 200°F (95°C). Line a rimmed baking sheet with paper towels. Pour oil to a depth of ¼ inch (6 mm) into a large nonstick frying pan and heat over medium-high heat until hot and shimmering but not smoking.

5 Working in batches to avoid crowding, fry the cakes, turning once, until golden brown and crispy, 2–3 minutes per side. Transfer to the prepared baking sheet to drain and keep warm in the oven. Repeat to cook the remaining cakes, adding a little more oil to the pan, if needed.

6 Arrange the cakes on a platter, sprinkle with salt, and serve.

# Desserts

# SSC Brownies

*Makes 15 large or 30 small brownies*

People always ask what makes these brownies so good. The answer is simple: crunchy, crispy rice cereal (thank you, Claude)! These brownies freeze well, staying fresh tightly wrapped in the freezer for up to 1 month, and thaw quickly for an almost-instant homemade dessert. Keep a stash handy.

**Nonstick cooking spray or unsalted butter for greasing**

**1 cup (8 oz/250 g) cold unsalted butter, cut into small cubes**

**2 cups (12 oz/375 g) semisweet chocolate chips, plus 1 cup (6 oz/185 g)**

**4 oz (125 g) bittersweet chocolate, chopped**

**3 large eggs**

**1 cup (8 oz/250 g) sugar**

**1 tbsp pure vanilla extract**

**¾ cup (4 oz/125 g) all-purpose flour**

**1 tsp baking powder**

**½ tsp kosher salt**

**¾ cup (1½ oz/45 g) crisped rice cereal (optional)**

1  Preheat the oven to 375°F (190°C). Lightly spray or grease a 9-by-12-inch (23-by-30-cm) baking pan with cooking spray or butter.

2  Combine the butter, the 2 cups chocolate chips, and the bittersweet chocolate in a metal bowl or the top pan of a double boiler and place over (not touching) simmering water. Heat, stirring, until all of the chocolate is melted and the mixture is smooth. Remove from the heat and let cool until still warm but not too hot to touch, about 5 minutes.

3  In a large bowl, combine the eggs, sugar, and vanilla and stir until well blended. Pour the egg mixture slowly into the warm chocolate mixture, stirring until thoroughly combined. Let cool to room temperature, about 15 minutes.

4  In a medium bowl, stir together the flour, baking powder, salt, the remaining 1 cup chocolate chips, and the crisped rice cereal, if using. Add to the cooled chocolate mixture and stir just until combined. Be careful not to overmix. Pour the batter into the prepared pan and smooth the top with a rubber spatula.

5  Bake just until a toothpick inserted into the center comes out clean, about 35–40 minutes. Be careful not to overbake. Transfer to a wire rack and let cool completely in the pan, then refrigerate until well chilled, about 4 hours. Cut into bars and serve. Store leftover bars in an airtight container at room temperature for up to 3 days.

# CHOCOLATE CHIP COOKIES

*Makes about 24 cookies*

Some say it's the chocolate, others say it's the butter, and still others say it's how you beat the dough. We say, brown sugar is the key to a good chocolate chip cookie, and these cookies are persuasive evidence. Serve warm out of the oven with a glass of cold milk. No one will turn down the offer.

1¼ cups (6½ oz/200 g) all-purpose flour

¾ tsp baking soda

½ tsp kosher salt

½ cup (4 oz/125 g) plus 2 tbsp unsalted butter, at room temperature

¾ cup (6 oz/185 g) firmly packed golden brown sugar

⅓ cup (3 oz/90 g) granulated sugar

1 large egg

1 tsp pure vanilla extract

2 cups (12 oz/375 g) semisweet chocolate chips

1  In a bowl, stir together the flour, baking soda, and salt. Set aside.

2  In a large bowl, using an electric mixer set on high speed, beat together the butter and sugars until pale and fluffy, 2–3 minutes. Add the egg and beat until the mixture is creamy, about 1 minute. Beat in the vanilla. Reduce the speed to low and mix in the flour mixture just until incorporated. Fold in the chocolate chips. Tightly cover and refrigerate the dough overnight.

3  Preheat the oven to 375°F (190°C). Line a large baking sheet with parchment paper. Using a spoon, place heaping tablespoons of the cold dough about 2 inches (5 cm) apart on the prepared baking sheet.

4  Bake until golden brown and puffy, 12–15 minutes. Transfer the cookies to a wire rack and let cool slightly before serving. Store fully cooled cookies in an airtight container at room temperature for up to 3 days.

# OATMEAL CRANBERRY COOKIES

*Makes about 18 cookies*

These cookies may fool you! They taste just like "regular" cookies but provide a sweet treat for anyone who needs to eat gluten-free, or prefers a low-gluten or vegan diet. But more importantly, for everyone who loves cookies, they're moist and simply delicious. The brown rice flour adds a nutty fullness.

**1 cup (3 oz/90 g) old-fashioned rolled oats**

**¾ cup (4 oz/125 g) brown rice flour**

**½ cup (2 oz/60 g) sweetened shredded coconut**

**2 tsp ground cinnamon**

**½ tsp kosher salt**

**½ cup (5½ oz/170 g) pure maple syrup**

**¼ cup (2 fl oz/60 ml) plus 2 tbsp canola oil**

**1 tsp pure vanilla extract**

**¼ cup (1 oz/30 g) dried cranberries**

**1** Preheat the oven to 350°F (180°C). Line a large baking sheet with parchment paper.

**2** In a bowl, stir together the oats, flour, coconut, cinnamon, and salt. In another bowl, whisk together the maple syrup, oil, and vanilla. Pour the wet ingredients over the dry ingredients and stir just until all of the dry ingredients are moistened. Fold in the cranberries.

**3** Using a tablespoon, place heaping tablespoons of the dough about 2 inches (5 cm) apart on the prepared baking sheet. Gently shape into rounds and push down on each mound with the back of the spoon.

**4** Bake until golden brown, 12–15 minutes. Transfer the cookies to a wire rack and let cool slightly before serving. Store fully cooled cookies in an airtight container at room temperature for up to 3 days.

# MINI BANANA BREAD MUFFINS

*Makes 24 mini muffins*

Bananas are famous for their potassium content: one banana can provide as much as 25 percent of the recommended daily dose for good health. But they are also a good source of fiber and other vitamins. Kids will love these sweet-but-not-too-sweet bite-sized banana breads. The portions are perfect for lunch boxes and moms' handbags. Use very ripe bananas for the best results.

**6 tbsp (3 oz/90 g) unsalted butter, melted, plus more for greasing**

**2 ripe bananas**

**¾ cup (6 oz/185 g) sugar**

**2 large eggs, beaten**

**1 tsp pure vanilla extract**

**1 tsp baking soda**

**½ tsp kosher salt**

**⅔ cup (3½ oz/105 g) all-purpose flour**

1 Preheat the oven to 375°F (190°C). Lightly grease a nonstick 24-cup mini muffin pan with butter.

2 In a large bowl, mash the bananas with a fork. Pour in the butter. Using a wooden spoon, stir until well blended. Add the sugar, eggs, and vanilla and stir to mix well. Sprinkle in the baking soda and salt and stir to mix, then stir in the flour just until combined. Be careful not to overmix the batter.

3 Using a spoon, gently drop the batter into the prepared muffin cups, filling each cup almost to the rim.

4 Bake until puffy and golden brown, 20–25 minutes. Let the muffins cool in the pan on a wire rack for about 5 minutes, then turn the muffins out onto the rack and serve warm or let cool. Store fully cooled muffins in an airtight container at room temperature for up to 4 days.

# APPLE PIE BARS

*Makes 18 bars*

These bars are a great choice to bring to a school bake sale or class party. They offer more nutrition than a typical cookie or brownie. The combination of flavors—warm Granny Smith apples, cinnamon, and oats—will make everyone's mouth water. Store in the refrigerator in an airtight container for up to 3 days.

**CRUST**

Nonstick cooking spray

1 cup (8 oz/250 g) unsalted butter, at room temperature

⅓ cup (3 oz/90 g) granulated sugar

1½ cups (7½ oz/235 g) all-purpose flour

¼ tsp kosher salt

**FILLING**

3 tbsp unsalted butter

¼ cup (2 oz/60 g) firmly packed golden brown sugar

4 large Granny Smith apples, about 1 lb (500 g) total weight, peeled, halved, cored, and thinly sliced

2 tsp ground cinnamon

¼ tsp freshly grated nutmeg

Crumble Topping (page 187)

1  To make the crust, preheat the oven to 375°F (190°C). Lightly spray a 9-by-12-inch (23-by-30-cm) baking pan with cooking spray.

2  In a large bowl, using an electric mixer set on high speed, beat together the butter and granulated sugar until pale and fluffy, about 2 minutes. Reduce the speed to low and beat in about ½ cup (2½ oz/75 g) of the flour and the salt, then add the remaining flour gradually and beat until the dough comes together into a soft ball. Transfer the dough to the prepared pan and, using your hands and a gentle touch, spread it out evenly over the bottom and slightly up the sides. Bake until the top is golden brown, 15–20 minutes. Transfer to a wire rack and let cool completely. Leave the oven on.

3  To make the filling, place the butter and brown sugar in a large frying pan. Place over low heat and, using a wooden spoon, stir to melt the sugar into the butter to form a syrup. Add the apples, toss to coat with the syrup, and raise the heat to medium-high. Cook, stirring often, until the apples have softened and are beginning to caramelize in the syrup, 15–20 minutes. If the pan begins to burn, sprinkle in a little water, scrape the pan bottom, and reduce the heat. When the apples are very soft, stir in the cinnamon and nutmeg. Remove from the heat and let cool completely.

4  Spread the apple filling over the baked crust in an even layer. Sprinkle the topping over and press lightly. Bake until the topping is golden, about 20 minutes. Let cool completely on a wire rack, then cut into bars and serve.

# BRENDA'S MINI PUMPKIN CUPCAKES

*Makes 24 mini cupcakes*

A delightful treat on a crisp autumn day, these festive mini cupcakes are our most popular dessert. The cream cheese frosting is just perfect, not too sweet and not too tart. Thank you Mary's mom, Brenda!

½ cup (4 fl oz/125 ml) canola oil, plus more for greasing

1 cup (5 oz/155 g) all-purpose flour

1 tsp baking powder

½ tsp baking soda

¼ tsp kosher salt

1 tsp ground cinnamon

½ can (7½ oz/235 g) pumpkin purée

1 cup (8 oz/250 g) sugar

2 large eggs, beaten

SSC Frosting (page 187)

1 Preheat the oven to 375°F (190°C). Lightly grease a nonstick 24-cup mini muffin pan with oil.

2 In a medium bowl, stir together the flour, baking powder, baking soda, salt, and cinnamon. In a large bowl, combine the pumpkin, sugar, eggs, and oil and stir until well blended. Add the dry ingredients to the wet ingredients and mix until thoroughly combined.

3 Using a small spoon, drop the batter into the prepared muffin cups, filling each cup almost to the rim. Bake until puffy and the top springs back when lightly touched, 15–20 minutes. Let cool in the pan on a wire rack for about 5 minutes, then turn the cupcakes out onto the rack and let cool completely.

4 Frost the cooled cupcakes with the frosting and serve. Store leftover cupcakes in an airtight container in the refrigerator for up to 3 days.

# MINI CHOCOLATE CUPCAKES WITH SSC FROSTING

*Makes 24 mini cupcakes*

Replace your everyday birthday cake with a couple dozen of these cupcakes—either chocolate or vanilla—and decorate them with fun colored sprinkles. Or better yet, let the kids decorate them. Children enjoy eating cupcakes out of hand more than they like to wrangle with a slice of cake on a plate, and the portion size is just right for small bellies. For the vanilla batter, see page 187.

**6 tbsp (3 oz/90 g) unsalted butter, at room temperature, plus more for greasing**

**1 cup (5 oz/155 g) all-purpose flour**

**⅓ cup (1 oz/30 g) unsweetened cocoa powder**

**1 tsp baking powder**

**¼ tsp kosher salt**

**¾ cup (6 oz/185 g) sugar**

**1 large egg**

**1 tsp pure vanilla extract**

**⅓ cup (2½ oz/75 g) sour cream**

**⅓ cup (3 fl oz/80 ml) whole milk**

**¼ cup (1½ oz/45 g) semisweet chocolate chips**

**SSC Frosting (page 187)**

1 Preheat the oven to 375°F (190°C). Lightly grease a nonstick 24-cup mini muffin pan with butter.

2 Sift together the flour, cocoa powder, baking powder, and salt into a large bowl. Set aside. In a stand mixer fitted with the paddle attachment, beat together the butter and sugar on medium-high speed until pale and fluffy, about 4 minutes. Add the egg and beat until incorporated. Beat in the vanilla. Reduce the speed to low and add the flour mixture in 3 batches alternately with the sour cream and milk in 2 batches, beginning and ending with the flour mixture and beating just until combined. Fold in the chocolate chips.

3 Using a small spoon, drop the batter into the prepared muffin cups, filling each cup about half full. Bake until the tops are puffed and a toothpick inserted into the center of a cupcake comes out clean, about 15 minutes. Let cool in the pan on a wire rack for about 10 minutes, then run a small, thin knife around the cups to loosen the tops. Turn the cupcakes out onto the rack and let cool completely.

4 Frost the cooled cupcakes with the frosting and serve. Store leftover cupcakes in an airtight container in the refrigerator for up to 3 days.

# SUMMER COBBLER

*Serves 6–8*

This cobbler celebrates summer, but you can adjust the recipe throughout the year to feature favorite seasonal fruits. Here, mixed berries provide plenty of the antioxidants that are important to maintaining good health. Susie's Tip: To divide the dough evenly, first split it in half, then cut each half into 6 equal pieces.

**BISCUITS**

3½ cups (17½ oz/545 g) all-purpose flour, plus more for dusting

1 tbsp baking powder

1 tsp kosher salt

1 cup (8 oz/250 g) cold unsalted butter, cut into small cubes

1¼ cups (10 fl oz/310 ml) whole milk

**FILLING**

1 cup (8 oz/250 g) sugar, plus more for sprinkling

⅓ cup (1½ oz/45 g) cornstarch

1 tsp kosher salt

Grated zest and juice of 1 lemon

2 pints (1 lb/500 g) strawberries, hulled and quartered

1 pint (½ lb/250 g) each raspberries, blueberries, and blackberries

2 tbsp heavy cream

Vanilla ice cream or whipped cream for serving

1 Preheat the oven to 375°F (190°C).

2 To make the biscuits, in a large bowl, stir together the flour, baking powder, and salt. Scatter the butter pieces on top and pinch into the flour mixture with your fingertips. Continue to pinch and toss until the mixture has the consistency of a uniform coarse, sandy meal. Add the milk and stir with a wooden spoon just until combined and a moist dough forms. Turn the dough out onto a lightly floured work surface and divide into 12 equal pieces.

3 To make the filling, in another large bowl, whisk together the sugar, cornstarch, salt, and lemon zest and juice. Add all of the berries and toss gently until well combined (hands work best). Pour the filling into a 9-by-12-inch (23-by-30-cm) baking dish and spread in an even layer. Arrange the biscuits on top of the filling, spacing them evenly. Brush each biscuit lightly with the cream and sprinkle with sugar.

4 Bake until the biscuits are golden brown and the filling is bubbling, 45–50 minutes. Remove from the oven and let cool for about 15 minutes. Serve warm with vanilla ice cream or whipped cream.

# MINI BLUEBERRY MUFFINS

*Makes 24 mini muffins*

These mini muffins will have you finishing off the crumbs without guilt. We make them with nonfat yogurt instead of butter, which significantly reduces the fat count. Despite that health-savvy substitution, they are moist and full of flavor. Don't forget to treat yourself to a sprinkle of brown sugar on top.

¼ cup (2 fl oz/60 ml) canola oil, plus more for greasing

1 cup (5 oz/155 g) all-purpose flour

1 tsp baking powder

½ tsp baking soda

¼ tsp kosher salt

½ cup (4 oz/125 g) plus 2 tbsp granulated sugar

1 large egg, beaten

¾ cup (6 oz/185 g) nonfat plain yogurt

Fresh or frozen blueberries for topping

2 tbsp firmly packed golden brown sugar

1 Preheat the oven to 375°F (190°C). Lightly grease a nonstick 24-cup mini muffin pan with oil.

2 Sift together the flour, baking powder, baking soda, and salt into a medium bowl and set aside. In a large bowl, combine the granulated sugar, egg, yogurt, and oil and stir until well blended. Add the dry ingredients to the wet ingredients and stir just until combined. Be careful not to overmix.

3 Using a small spoon, drop the batter into the prepared muffin cups, filling each cup only half full. Arrange 3–4 blueberries on top of each muffin, poking them gently partway into the batter but leaving them exposed. Sprinkle the tops generously with the brown sugar.

4 Bake until puffy and golden brown, 20–25 minutes. Let cool in the pan on a wire rack for about 5 minutes, then turn the muffins out onto the rack and serve warm, or let cool completely. Store fully cooled muffins in an airtight container in the refrigerator for up to 3 days.

# SARAH'S CHERRY-ALMOND SCONES

*Makes 12 scones*

These not-too-sweet scones are a Sarah Flynn specialty. We love how light, flaky, and lemony they are. What else could you want in a scone? Use dried apricots for a variation. Serve these at breakfast, as dessert, or as a snack anytime.

½ cup (2 oz/60 g) sliced almonds

2 tbsp sugar, plus ⅓ cup (3 oz/90 g)

2 tbsp fresh lemon juice

2¼ cups (9 oz/280 g) all-purpose flour, plus more for dusting

1 tbsp baking powder

1 tbsp grated lemon zest

1 tsp salt

¾ cup (6 oz/185 g) cold unsalted butter, cut into small cubes

½ cup (2 oz/60 g) dried cherries, coarsely chopped

¾ cup (6 fl oz/180 ml) cold half-and-half, plus more if needed

1 Preheat the oven to 375°F (190°C). Line a large baking sheet with parchment paper and set aside.

2 Spread the almonds in a single layer on another rimmed baking sheet. Toast in the oven, stirring once, until lightly golden and fragrant, 5–7 minutes. Transfer immediately to a plate and let cool completely. Leave the oven on.

3 In a small bowl, whisk together the 2 tbsp sugar and 1 tbsp of the lemon juice until smooth. Set aside for the glaze.

4 In a large bowl, whisk together the flour, the remaining ⅓ cup sugar, the baking powder, the lemon zest, and the salt. Scatter the butter pieces on top and pinch into the flour mixture with your fingertips. Continue to pinch and toss until the mixture has the consistency of a uniform coarse, sandy meal. Stir in the cherries and almonds.

5 Pour the half-and-half and the remaining 1 tbsp lemon juice over the dough. Using a fork, stir gently just until the dough comes together in moist clumps, sprinkling in a little more half-and-half if the dough seems dry. Do not overwork the dough.

6 Dust your hands and a work surface with flour. Gather the dough into a ball, then divide it in half. Flatten each half into a disk about 6 inches (15 cm) in diameter. Cut each disk into 6 wedges. Arrange the wedges on the parchment-lined baking sheet and brush with the glaze.

7 Bake until the tops and edges are lightly golden, 20–25 minutes. Transfer the scones to wire racks and serve warm.

# POACHED PEARS WITH WARM CHOCOLATE SAUCE

*Serves 4–6*

We love this easy, refreshing fruit dessert that offers a healthy alternative to some of the more typical, and richer, favorites. The chocolate sauce adds a sweetly nuanced and special finish. The poaching liquid for the pears can be saved and reused a second time; the cinnamon-spiced flavor only deepens and becomes more aromatic as it reduces further.

**3 cups (24 fl oz/750 ml) water**

**1 cup (8 fl oz/250 ml) apple cider**

**2½ cups (20 oz/625 g) sugar**

**Grated zest of 1 lemon**

**Grated zest of 1 orange**

**1 tsp ground cinnamon or 1 whole cinnamon stick**

**1 tsp pure vanilla extract**

**¼ tsp kosher salt**

**4–6 ripe but firm Bosc, Seckel, or Anjou pears, peeled but stems intact**

### CHOCOLATE SAUCE

**1 cup (8 fl oz/250 ml) heavy cream**

**2 cups (12 oz/375 g) semisweet chocolate chips**

**1 tbsp clover honey**

1 In a saucepan, combine the water, cider, sugar, lemon and orange zests, cinnamon, vanilla, and salt over medium-high heat. Bring to a simmer, stirring to dissolve the sugar. Reduce the heat to medium-low, add the pears, and poach, turning several times, until they are honey colored and tender, 35–40 minutes. For the best flavor, let the pears cool completely in the poaching liquid.

2 Meanwhile, make the chocolate sauce: In a small saucepan, bring the cream to a simmer over medium heat. Place the chocolate chips in a heatproof bowl and drizzle the honey on top. Holding a fine-mesh sieve over the bowl of chocolate, pour in the hot cream. Whisk until the chocolate melts and the cream is fully incorporated.

3 Arrange the whole pears on dessert plates. Or, carefully cut each pear in half lengthwise and scoop out the cores with the tip of a small spoon or a melon baller and then place on dessert plates. Drizzle the warm pears with the chocolate sauce or serve the sauce in small individual bowls alongside.

# Lemon Mousse

*Serves 6–8*

This sweet-tart "no-bake"—and no-fuss—dessert is great for a dinner party because it's best served the day after you make it. Spoon it into a big, pretty glass bowl or divide it among individual bowls or stemmed glasses. Serve topped with fresh berries, if you like, and accompany with a piece of shortbread or a favorite store-bought cookie. Kids will love its airy texture.

**1 cup (8 oz/250 g) plus 1 tbsp sugar**

**2 tbsp grated lemon zest, plus more for garnish**

**¾ cup (6 fl oz/180 ml) fresh lemon juice**

**6 large egg yolks**

**2 large whole eggs**

**2 cups (16 fl oz/500 ml) cold heavy cream**

**1** In a large metal bowl, combine the sugar, lemon zest and juice, egg yolks, and whole eggs and whisk until blended. Set the bowl over (not touching) gently simmering water in a saucepan. Whisk the mixture constantly until it thickens and develops a curdlike texture, 5–8 minutes. Remove from the heat and let cool slightly, then refrigerate, uncovered, until cooled completely, about 2 hours.

**2** Place the cream in a bowl. Using an electric mixer set on medium speed, beat until medium-firm peaks form. Fold one-third of the whipped cream into the cooled curd to lighten it, then fold in the remaining cream just until no streaks remain.

**3** Divide the mousse among individual bowls or glasses or transfer to a large clear-glass bowl. Cover tightly and refrigerate until well chilled and set, at least 4 hours or up to overnight. Garnish with a little lemon zest and serve.

# FROZEN FRUIT POPS

*Each recipe makes 6 ice pops*

This is a fun and fast summer recipe that is both light and refreshing.
Mix and match your favorite fruits and herbs. We like using mint and basil
for their sweet tones and invigorating aromas. Susie's Tip: Use ice-cube trays
and tongue depressors from the drugstore if you don't have the molds.
Add the tongue depressors after the ice pops have begun to set.

**SIMPLE SYRUP**

**1 cup (8 oz/250 g) sugar**

**½ cup (4 fl oz/125 ml) water**

**PINEAPPLE-MINT POPS**

**2 tbsp simple syrup**

**6 cups (2¼ lb/1.2 kg) cubed fresh pineapple, plus juices from cutting**

**¼ cup (2 fl oz/60 ml) water**

**6 large fresh mint leaves**

**Small pinch of kosher salt**

**STRAWBERRY-WATERMELON-BASIL POPS**

**2 tbsp simple syrup**

**2 cups (8 oz/250 g) hulled and quartered strawberries**

**4 cups (1¼ lb/625 g) peeled and cubed seedless watermelon, plus juices from cutting**

**¼ cup (2 fl oz/60 ml) water**

**6 large fresh basil leaves**

**Small pinch of kosher salt**

**1** To make the simple syrup, in a small saucepan, combine the sugar and water over medium-high heat. Bring to a simmer, stirring until the sugar is completely dissolved, about 5 minutes. Remove from the heat and let cool. You should have 1 cup (8 fl oz/250 ml). Store unused simple syrup in the refrigerator in a tightly covered jar for up to 2 weeks.

**2** To make the pops, combine all the ingredients for the recipe of your choice in a blender or food processor and process until the fruit is entirely puréed and the mixture resembles a frothy juice. Taste and adjust the seasoning, adding a tiny bit more salt if the flavors seem to need a boost or more simple syrup for a sweeter ice pop.

**3** Pour the ice-pop base into a standard 6-section ice-pop mold, 2 standard ice-cube trays, or any molds of your choice.

**4** If using an ice-pop mold, freeze until completely set, at least 4 hours. If using ice-cube trays, freeze for about 1 hour and then insert wooden sticks or short skewers into the center of each pop and freeze until completely set, about 1 hour longer.

# BASIC RECIPES

## PIZZA DOUGH

Makes four 6-inch (15-cm) pizzas

**1 cup (8 fl oz/250 ml) warm water (105°–115°F/40°–46°C)**

**1½ tsp active dry yeast**

**½ tsp sugar**

**2 cups (10 oz/315 g) all-purpose flour, plus more for dusting**

**1½ tsp salt**

**Olive oil for greasing**

Pour the warm water into a large bowl. Sprinkle the yeast and sugar over the water. Let stand until the yeast is foamy, about 1 minute. Stir until the yeast dissolves.

Add the flour and salt to the yeast mixture and stir until a soft dough forms. Turn the dough out onto a lightly floured work surface and knead until smooth and elastic, about 10 minutes, dusting with more flour as needed. The dough should be soft but not sticky.

Lightly grease a large bowl with oil. Put the dough in the bowl and turn to coat with the oil. Cover the bowl with a kitchen towel, place in a warm, draft-free place, and let the dough rise until it doubles in size, about 1 hour.

Divide the dough into 4 equal pieces and shape each piece into a disk. Place on a lightly oiled baking sheet, cover with plastic wrap again, and let rise until doubled, about 30 minutes longer. Roll out, top, and bake as directed in individual recipes. The dough can be tightly wrapped and stored in the refrigerator for up to 2 weeks or in the freezer for up to 1 month.

## FRESH PASTA DOUGH

Makes 1 lb (500 g)

**2 cups (10 oz/315 g) all-purpose or semolina flour, plus more for dusting**

**½ tsp kosher salt**

**3 large eggs**

**Olive oil for greasing**

In a food processor, combine the flour and salt and pulse to mix. With the machine running, add the eggs one at a time, waiting until each is fully incorporated before adding the next. Process just until a coarse and mealy dough forms. Stop the machine and pinch a small portion of the dough between your fingers; it should hold together.

Turn the dough out onto a lightly floured work surface and gather it into a ball. Knead until smooth and elastic, about 7 minutes, dusting with more flour as needed to prevent sticking. Lightly grease a bowl with oil, place the dough ball in the bowl, and turn the dough to coat with the oil. Cover with plastic wrap and let rest for about 30 minutes.

Divide the dough in half. Press each half into a disc about 1 inch (2.5 cm) thick. Set a pasta machine to the widest setting and roll 1 dough piece through the rollers. Fold the sheet into thirds, lightly dust with flour, and roll through the widest setting again, seam side first. Turn the dial to the next narrowest setting and fold and roll the sheet in the same manner twice. Repeat with each progressively narrower setting, rolling twice, up to and including the second-narrowest setting. Be sure to dust the sheet lightly with flour before every pass, and use your hands and arms to support the sheet as it lengthens. Set the finished sheet aside on a floured work surface and repeat to roll out the second dough piece.

Let the sheets rest for about 15 minutes, then prepare and use as directed in individual recipes.

## SSC Gnocchi

Makes 25 dumplings

4 large russet potatoes, about 2 lb (1 kg) total weight, peeled and cut into 1-inch (2.5-cm) cubes

6 large egg yolks

2 tbsp olive oil

1 tsp kosher salt

Grated zest of 3 Meyer lemons

1½ cups (7½ oz/235 g) all-purpose flour, sifted, plus more for dusting

To make the gnocchi, put the potatoes in a saucepan and add cold water to cover. Bring to a boil over high heat, then reduce the heat to medium and simmer until the potatoes are very tender, 8–12 minutes. Drain the potatoes, then return them to the warm pan and stir over low heat to dry the potatoes out, about 30 seconds.

Pass the potatoes through a ricer onto a large rimmed baking sheet and spread in an even layer to cool. In a small bowl, whisk together the egg yolks, oil, salt, and lemon zest. Pour the egg mixture evenly over the potatoes. Sprinkle the flour evenly over the top. Using a fork, stir gently until well mixed and a rough dough forms.

Gather the dough into a ball and transfer to a well-floured work surface. Knead gently, dusting with flour as needed to prevent sticking or if the dough seems too wet, until soft and fluffy, 3–5 minutes.

Divide the dough into 4 equal pieces. Lightly flour your hands. Working with 1 dough piece at a time, roll it with your palms into a rope about ½ inch (12 mm) in diameter and 10 inches (25 cm) long. Cut the rope into 1½-inch (4-cm) pieces and transfer to a lightly floured baking sheet. Repeat with the remaining dough pieces. Transfer to the refrigerator and chill to set for about 15 minutes.

Remove the gnocchi from the refrigerator. Holding a fork with the tines facing down, roll each gnocchi down the fork to form a little squarish dumpling marked with ridges (this will help grab the sauce). Use as directed in individual recipes.

## Homemade Tomato Sauce

Makes 6 cups (48 fl oz/1.5 l)

2 tablespoons olive oil

4 garlic cloves, minced

1 cup (4 oz/125 g) chopped yellow onion

½ cup (3 oz/90 g) coarsely grated or thinly sliced carrots

Fresh thyme sprigs

2 cans (28 oz/875 g each) plum tomatoes, preferably San Marzano, with their juices

1 teaspoon kosher salt

½ teaspoon freshly ground pepper

In a saucepan over medium heat, sauté the garlic and onion in the olive oil until soft and beginning to color, 10–12 minutes. Add the carrots and thyme and sauté until the carrots are soft, about 5 minutes.

Add the tomatoes and their juices and crush with a fork to release their flavor. Stir in the salt and pepper. Bring the sauce to a boil and reduce to a simmer. Cover and simmer for 1 hour. Allow the sauce to cool for about 15 minutes, then puree in batches in a blender. Adjust the seasoning if necessary and let cool. The tomato sauce will keep, tightly covered in the refrigerator, for up to 3 weeks.

## Pesto

Makes 1 cup (8 oz/250 g)

1 bunch fresh basil

2 cloves garlic

2 tbsp pine nuts, toasted

½ cup (4 fl oz/125 ml) olive oil

½ cup (2 oz/60 g) grated Parmesan cheese

Discard the tough stems from the basil. In a food processor or blender, combine the basil, garlic, pine nuts, and olive oil and process until smooth. Add the Parmesan and pulse briefly to blend. Transfer the pesto to a bowl, cover, and refrigerate until ready to use.

## HOMEMADE KETCHUP

Makes 3½ cups (28 oz/875 g)

**2 tbsp vegetable oil**

**1 yellow onion, finely chopped**

**1 can (28 oz/875 g) plum tomatoes, preferably San Marzano, with their juices**

**1 tbsp tomato paste**

**1 cup (7 oz/220 g) firmly packed golden brown sugar**

**½ cup (4 fl oz/125 ml) cider vinegar**

**½ tsp kosher salt**

Heat the oil in a heavy-bottomed saucepan over medium heat. Add the onion and cook until softened, about 5 minutes. Add the tomatoes and their juices and crush with a fork to release the flavor. Add the tomato paste, brown sugar, vinegar, and salt and stir to mix well.

Bring to a boil, then reduce the heat to maintain a very low simmer. Simmer uncovered, stirring occasionally, until very thick, about 1 hour. Stir more often at the end of cooking to prevent scorching.

Let cool slightly, then transfer the ketchup to a blender or food processor and process until smooth. Cover and refrigerate until well chilled and the flavors have developed, about 2 hours, before using. The ketchup will keep, tightly covered in the refrigerator, for up to 3 weeks.

## AVOCADO PUREÈ

Makes 1½ cups (12 oz/375 g)

**2 ripe avocados, pitted and peeled**

**½ cup (4 oz/125 g) sour cream**

**¼ cup (2 fl oz/60 ml) fresh lemon juice**

**2 tbsp fresh lime juice**

**1½ tsp kosher salt**

In a blender or food processor, combine all of the ingredients and process until smooth and creamy. Taste and adjust the seasoning. Use right away.

## SESAME-LIME VINAIGRETTE

Makes 4 cups (32 fl oz/1 l)

**¾ cup (6 fl oz/180 ml) fresh lime juice**

**¼ cup (2 fl oz/60 ml) seasoned rice vinegar**

**2 tbsp Dijon mustard**

**2 tbsp sugar**

**1½ tsp kosher salt**

**⅔ cup (5 fl oz/160 ml) Asian sesame oil**

In a blender, combine the lime juice, vinegar, mustard, sugar, and salt and blend briefly on high speed to mix. With the machine running on low speed, slowly add the sesame oil in a thin stream and blend until emulsified. Taste and adjust the seasoning. (The dressing can be made up to 1 week in advance and stored in a tightly covered jar in the refrigerator.)

## CREAMY PARMESAN DRESSING

Makes 2½ cups (20 fl oz/625 ml)

**1¼ cups (10 fl oz/310 ml) mayonnaise**

**½ cup (4 oz/125 g) sour cream**

**½ cup (2 oz/60 g) grated Parmesan cheese**

**2 cloves garlic, coarsely chopped**

**⅓ cup (½ oz/15 g) chopped fresh dill**

**Juice of 1 lemon**

**Freshly ground pepper**

**⅓ cup (3 fl oz/80 ml) olive oil**

In a blender, combine the mayonnaise, sour cream, Parmesan, garlic, dill, lemon juice, and a few grinds of pepper and blend on high speed to mince the garlic and mix well. With the machine running on low speed, add the olive oil in a thin stream and blend until emulsified. Pour into a bowl and taste and adjust the seasoning. Cover and refrigerate for 1 hour before serving. (The dressing can be made up to 1 week in advance and stored in a tightly covered jar in the refrigerator.)

## Ginger-Yogurt Marinade

Makes 3 cups (24 oz/750 g)

2 cups (1 lb/500 g) plain yogurt

6 cloves garlic, coarsely chopped

2 tbsp peeled and coarsely chopped
fresh ginger

3 tbsp fresh lemon juice

1 tbsp garam masala

1 tbsp smoked paprika

2 tsp mild chili powder

1 cup (1 oz/30 g) lightly packed
fresh cilantro leaves, chopped

Combine the yogurt, garlic, ginger, lemon juice, garam masala, smoked paprika, chili powder, and cilantro in a blender or food processor and process until smooth. Taste and adjust the seasoning. Cover and refrigerate until ready to use.

## Citrus Yogurt Dip

Makes 3 cups (24 fl oz/750 ml)

1 cup (8 oz/250 g) plain yogurt

1½ cups (12 fl oz/375 ml) water

½ cup (4 oz/125 g) sour cream

1 tbsp chopped fresh chives

1 tbsp chopped fresh basil

1 tbsp chopped fresh cilantro

1 tsp kosher salt

¼ tsp freshly ground pepper

Grated zest and juice from 1 lemon

In a bowl, combine all of the ingredients and stir to mix well. Taste and adjust the seasoning. Cover and refrigerate until ready to serve.

## Sweet Chile Dipping Sauce

Makes 1½ cups (12 fl oz/375 ml)

1 cup (8 fl oz/250 ml) mayonnaise

2 tbsp Thai sweet chile sauce

2 cloves garlic, minced

2 tbsp peeled and grated fresh ginger

½ tsp kosher salt

In a small bowl, combine all of the ingredients and stir to mix well. Taste and adjust the seasoning. Cover and refrigerate until ready to serve.

## Applesauce

Makes 6 cups (48 fl oz/1.5 l)

1 lb (500 g) tart green apples,
such as Granny Smith

¾ tsp fresh lemon juice

¼ cup (2 fl oz/60 ml) apple cider

1 tbsp sugar

⅛ tsp ground cinnamon

Peel and core the apples, then cut into large chunks. Put them in a large, heavy-bottomed saucepan, drizzle with the lemon juice, and toss to coat. Add the cider and sprinkle with the sugar and cinnamon. Place the pan over medium heat and bring to a boil, stirring to dissolve the sugar. Reduce the heat to maintain a gentle simmer, cover, and cook until the apples are tender, about 20 minutes. Uncover and cook to allow any excess liquid to evaporate, about 5 minutes longer. Remove from the heat, let cool slightly, transfer to a food processor, and process to a smooth purée. Let cool completely, then refrigerate until serving.

## Vanilla Cupcake Batter

Makes 24 mini cupcakes

1 cup (5 oz/155 g) all-purpose flour

1 tsp baking powder

¼ tsp kosher salt

½ cup (4 fl oz/125 ml) whole milk

1 tsp pure vanilla extract

6 tbsp (3 oz/90 g) unsalted butter,
at room temperature

¾ cup (6 oz/185 g) sugar

1 large egg

In a large bowl, whisk together the flour, baking powder, and salt. In a small bowl, stir together the milk and vanilla. Set aside. In a stand mixer fitted with the paddle attachment, beat together the butter and sugar on medium-high speed until pale and fluffy, about 4 minutes. Add the egg and beat until incorporated. Reduce the speed to low and add the flour mixture in 3 parts alternately with the milk mixture in 2 parts, beginning and ending with the flour mixture and beating just until combined. To prepare the cupcakes, see page 171.

## SSC Frosting

Makes 2½ cups (24 oz/750 g)

1 cup (8 oz/250 g) cream cheese, softened

1 cup (8 oz/250 g) unsalted butter, softened

2 tsp pure vanilla extract

2 cups (8 oz/250 g) confectioners' sugar,
more if desired

In a mixer, beat the cream cheese and butter at high speed until light and fluffy, 3–4 minutes. Beat in the vanilla and reduce the speed to low. Stir in the sugar and mix until well combined. If lumpy, briefly increase the speed to high and mix until just smooth. Use as directed in individual recipes.

## Crumble Topping

Makes 2½ cups (15 oz/470 g)

1 cup (3 oz/90 g) quick-cooking rolled oats

½ cup (2½ oz/75 g) plus 2 tbsp all-purpose flour

½ cup (3½ oz/105 g) firmly packed
golden brown sugar

½ tsp ground cinnamon

¼ tsp baking soda

¼ tsp kosher salt

½ cup (4 oz/125 g) cold unsalted butter,
cut into small cubes

¼ cup (1 oz/30 g) walnuts, toasted and
coarsely chopped

In a large bowl, stir together the oats, flour, brown sugar, cinnamon, baking soda, and salt. Scatter the butter pieces on top and pinch into the oats mixture with your fingertips. Continue to pinch and toss until the mixture comes together into uniform coarse, sandy clumps. Stir in the walnuts and refrigerate until ready to use.

# INDEX

# weldon**owen**

415 Jackson Street, Suite 200, San Francisco, CA 94111
Telephone: 415 291 0100  Fax: 415 291 8841
www.wopublishing.com

**THE SUPPER CLUB**

Conceived and produced by Weldon Owen, Inc.

**A WELDON OWEN PRODUCTION**

Copyright © 2011 by Susie's Supper Club, LLC
Photographs © 2011 by Con Poulos
All rights reserved, including the right of
reproduction in whole or in part in any form.

Color separations by Embassy Graphics in Canada
Printed and bound by 1010 Printing in China

First printed in 2011

10 9 8 7 6 5 4 3 2

Library of Congress Control Number: 2001012345

ISBN-13: 978-1-61628-115-1
ISBN-10: 1-61628-115-4

Weldon Owen is a division of
## BONNIER

**WELDON OWEN, INC.**

CEO and President  Terry Newell
VP, Sales and Marketing  Amy Kaneko
Director of Finance  Mark Perrigo

VP and Publisher  Hannah Rahill
Associate Publisher  Amy Marr
Assistant Editor  Becky Duffett

Creative Director  Emma Boys
Art Director  Kara Church

Production Director  Chris Hemesath
Production Manager  Michelle Duggan
Color Manager  Teri Bell

Photographer  Con Poulos
Food Stylist  Alison Attenborough

## ACKNOWLEDGMENTS

**From Susie Cover:** I would like to thank Mary May, Emma Mcmahon, and Sarah Flynn who
helped develop these recipes, especially Sarah, who tirelessly re-tested these recipes with me.

Thank you to Kim Witherspoon and Amy Marr for making this book happen.

Thanks to Con Poulos for his transcendent photos, which have represented SSC since its inception.

To the SSC moms and my partners in crime, Marcia Mishaan and Samantha Schlumberger: Thanks Marcia for your
incredible enthusiasm, ideas, and keeping us laughing. Thank you Samantha for your hard work and stunning design,
which is beautifully displayed throughout this book, our packaging, and everywhere you see the SSC brand.

To Andy for all the cooking and all the laughs, and Brad and Max for charades and Monday dinners.

To my mother, Mary, for her never-ending support and love; to Rick, Alice, and Madeline, for my heart.

And a special thanks to Claude Wasserstein, without whom SSC would simply not exist.
For your generosity, partnership, and friendship, I thank you.

Also love to my father Franklin, whom I miss cooking for every day.

To all the SSC members who ordered our food, gave us feedback, and supported
us throughout the years, my deep appreciation and thanks.

**Weldon Owen** wishes to thank the following people for their generous support in producing this book:
Donita Boles, Kimberly Chun, Audrey Cullen, Christina Holmes, Julia Humes, Erin Kunkel, Carrie Neves,
Elizabeth Parson, Tatum Quon, Ryan Rice, Elena Rosen, and Sharon Silva.